The

Empowering
Church

How one congregation supports lay
people's ministries in the world

Davida Foy Crabtree

An Alban Institute Publication

The Publications Program of The Alban Institute is assisted by a grant from Trinity Church, New York City.

Library of Congress Catalog Card # 89-85376.

CONTENTS

Grateful acknowledgment is made for use of excerpts from "Some Notes on Planned Social Change," an unpublished paper by Jackson W. Carroll, 1978. Used by permission from the author.

ACKNOWLEDGMENTS

The members of Colchester Federated Church are the true authors of this work. It has been through our life together that the ideas and events drawn together here have come to have significance both for us and for others. This is their story, and I am indebted to their loving spirit, their openness to change, and their love of the faith.

This book was originally written as a Doctor of Ministry dissertation at Hartford Seminary. Hartford's commitment to excellence in the reflective practice of ministry in and through congregations gave me the courage to try some things that haven't been tried much before in mainline churches. Their collegial style of education and careful attention to sociological dimensions of ministry were invaluable throughout the program.

Finally, I give God thanks for my family: especially for my husband, David Hindinger, who gives me both inspiration and grounding in the real world; and for my mother and my late father, Davida and Alfred Foy, a teacher and a typewriter mechanic respectively, who raised me in a home where Christian ministry was clearly everyone's work.

Davida Foy Crabtree
Colchester, Connecticut
July, 1989

The Empowering Church tells the story of Colchester (Connecticut) Federated Church and its effort to empower the ministries of the laity in their daily lives. This little book traces the church's expanding understanding over four years.

At first, the task seemed to be programmatic: how can we provide program that will help people make the connection between Sunday and Monday? We offered single-evening experiences, weekend retreats, and year-long support groups. We created vocational prayers and discussion starters for church committees. Our program has been both extensive and intensive.

After a while we began to see that our messages were contradicting each other. Preaching, worship, and program effectively communicated the biblical mandate to go out in ministry. The church's organizational systems and structures, however, encouraged members only to serve the institutional church. All that we were doing in our local congregation (and not only in Colchester!) focused on "holding-them-here" rather than "sending-them-out."

As we began to look at these mixed messages we saw that administrative committees predominated. Where there were mission and ministry committees, they focused on the corporate life of the church (local and denominational), not on empowering the members for ministry. Yet the Scriptures and church teaching emphasize the living out of the faith by the believer in her or his own life of ministry and action in the world.

One longtime member of the church, seeking to understand the program, commented, "It's what you're supposed to practice in your daily life that you've learned on Sunday. That's all it is." Yet most members have a difficult time making the connection between Sunday and Monday. The church must develop support systems to encourage its members to think in new ways about their lives and their practice of the Christian faith.

A few years later another member asked, "How do we connect the ministry of the laity with our structure and with everything we do in the church and outside the church?" It is the combination of these two comments from laity that this book addresses.

So, following up on program, we also developed a systemic approach to our concern. In this phase, we looked at every aspect of our organizational life and clarified its contribution to the empowerment of ministry. We examined existing committees and their responsibilities. We identified the essential components of effective support for the ministry of the laity and assigned responsibility for them to the appropriate committees. In other words, we created a "management system" for the church's work on the ministry of the laity.

Yet still the messages were mixed. The more we delved into the systemic questions, the clearer our need for restructuring became. If we truly wanted coherence in our teaching and our church life, we needed a structure that would embody the teaching. So now a new design for the entire structure of our church has been developed and is beginning to be introduced to the congregation.

It is important to note at the beginning that this work is ongoing. While the leaders of the church "own" the fundamental way of work described here, the whole church does not—yet. We are talking about profound change in the identity and mission of the local church. Such change takes enormous patience and perseverance.

What is described here is less a program of the church than it is a new way of being the church. It is a way that takes seriously not only the gathering of the church for worship and education, but also the scattering of the church for ministry in daily life. It takes seriously not only the program of the church, but its incarnation in organizational structure as well. It moves us toward intentional focus on the nurturing of persons in faith and in ministry as well as the strengthening of the institution for its mission and ministry.

While the breakthroughs in Colchester are exciting for those who have been involved, they are not a blueprint for other churches. Every congregation must struggle its own way through the questions and issues that confront its particular life. Congregational characteristics like the age of the membership, the nature of their employment, the size of their community are important to the designing of program, system, and structure. Our setting and denominational affiliations have affected the choices we have made. The results are not pure, but they are lived realities.

I have chosen to share this story as accurately as possible. There are points at which the way it happened differs from accepted practice of ministry. My strong leadership role in the beginning is a case in point. I too share the vision of a more collegial style which engages the laity in mutual ministry. It didn't happen that way at every point, however.

So I offer this account of our church's struggle to be faithful without any assumption that we have the answers. I only know that we have discovered some of the questions, and that wrestling with them can give new life to a church and its pastor.

Colchester Federated Church

"Where tradition meets tomorrow" says the sign as one exits from the highway in Colchester, Connecticut. The sign has meaning not only in relation to the town, but also in relation to the ministry of Colchester Federated Church.

Colchester itself is a traditional small New England town now experiencing rapid population growth as a third-ring suburb of five different cities in eastern and central Connecticut. Affordable starter homes are being supplanted by expensive executive homes. Machinists and welders are being edged out by middle-level managers and data base administrators. Gracious old homes lining the main streets of town are gradually becoming commercial office spaces rather than residences.

In the midst of all this change, in the very center of town facing the town green, sits the meetinghouse of the Federated Church, a symbol of tradition itself. The present building was erected in 1840, and the 1960 addition was constructed on the back of the building in such a way that it is hardly noticed from historic South Main Street. The meetinghouse is such a symbol of the town that it is featured on the town's seal and the commemorative dinner plates made from the design of that seal.

Twenty years ago a number of young families left this church to join in starting the local Bible Baptist Church. That event left the remaining members reluctant to talk about faith matters because they "might offend each other." Faith is understood as private. Because it was not discussed, it was neither strongly owned nor applied to the public arena. Today that exodus also means that this church has few members between the ages of 45 and 55. This fact offers both problem and opportunity. The problem is leadership, and to some extent stewardship. The opportunity is that of focusing on issues of vocation/occupation because of the relative youthfulness of much of the church membership.

This church is now a congregation of 610 members, formed in 1949 by the union of the Borough Baptist Church and the First Congregational Church. Baptists constitute about 13 percent of the congregation, United Church of Christ members about 67 percent. An additional 20 percent are members only of this congregation, an arrangement developed at the time of the federation for those who had been members of other denominations and wanted to maintain that identity. Their numbers have been decreasing significantly in the last eight years.

The activities described here were originally conceived to address three primary issues in the life of Colchester Federated Church: (1) the absence of an adult "owned" faith that could help members bridge the gap between Sunday worship and Monday life; (2) the development of an explicitly Christian leadership, particularly among the younger adults (age 18 to 40) who make up three-fifths of the congregation; and (3) the introduction of the public dimension of the faith in a way that could elicit personal commitment from the members.

In addition to these primary issues, the efforts described here have also consolidated work on adult education; the meaning of membership; the management of numerical growth; the introduction of ongoing small groups into the church's life; and gifts identification and human resource development.

However, as these programmatic dimensions were carried out, it became apparent that there were major issues facing all Christian churches that were being addressed here. In particular, there is a disjuncture between the stated purpose of the Christian church and the way it is organized locally. Form does not follow function. The church exists for mission, for the sake of the world. Yet it is organized to build itself up as an institution. It draws people to itself, but fails to send them back out. It blesses the work its members do within the institution, but pays no attention to the work they do "outside" the church.

Therefore, our church has chosen to go beyond the programmatic, to begin to address structural and systemic issues. When we conduct programs of any kind in the church, basically we are working at changing the culture of the institution. We are seeking to change persons and their interaction with one another. Whether those programs are Bible study, support or prayer groups, issue-focused or theology-focused, our intent and result is usually a change in the quality of life of the persons and the institution.

Change in the culture of an organization, however, is short-lived unless there is a concomitant change in structure and system. Likewise, change in structure and system is empty unless there is change in the culture as well.

Building on a programmatic base, then, as pastoral leader, I have sought to create a management system that can integrate and systematize multiple aspects of the church's life. It provides for planning and systematizing, for mobilizing resources, and for envisioning and leading functions, each an important component of management. Major elements of church life are addressed in the way they integrate support for the ministries of the laity: ministry support, membership, leadership, spiritual and personal growth, and structure, evaluation, and process.

When it is completely implemented, the management system will integrate program, process, and organizational structure into a coherent system supporting the ministry of the laity.

CHAPTER I

Program Supporting the Ministries of the Laity

For the last nine years, I have been the pastor of this church. Over all of that time, I have been preaching about the ministry of the laity. Sometimes I have been able to see the effect of all that proclamation. Often I have not. In the early years, I struggled with self-doubt because it seemed that no one got the message. Gradually as I proposed programs that supported the theme of my preaching, I began to see growth in understanding. As the programs intensified over the years, I began to see laity getting excited about ministry. Clearly the preaching message is an integral part of the program, but it can only be one part if we want the message to get through. Here is a brief summary of our program work.

In the spring of 1982, we held the first adult retreat this church had ever had. The theme was "Discovering our Gifts." In 1983, we formed our Parents' Center as an outreach ministry of advocacy, support, and education. In 1984, we launched the church's first planning process, which led to an organizational restructuring of the congregation's work, building in components that have had an influence on our present restructuring.

In 1985, we sponsored a conference entitled "Beyond a Sunday Christianity" and forty-eight persons participated, even though it landed on the same weekend as hurricane Gloria. This conference was led by a resource person from the Center for the Ministry of the Laity in Newton Centre, Massachusetts.

Conscious that a conference was a way of work comfortable for middle-class, educated persons but alien to working class, less verbally skilled people, we then shifted our approach. In the spring of 1986, we formed a "listening team" of three laity (a machinist, an executive, and a data base analyst), who invited occupational groups to spend an evening talking about their work.

We have a computerized record of the occupation of each member, so invitations to events like this are made easy.

Before the first evening session, the listening team spent many hours together, talking about their work lives and their faith issues. They developed a list of areas for discussion by the groups that included, for instance:

Describe how you spend your day.

What is satisfying for you in your work? What stressful?

What is the impact of your work on your health, on your family, on your financial life?

How does your workplace need to change? How can you help, or not?

What are the ethical and justice or fairness issues you have to deal with at work?

Does it make any difference that you are a Christian in your workplace? How does your faith connect to your work?

As pastor, I served as silent observer-recorder. Office workers, teachers, and production workers expressed their satisfactions and stresses about their work. In every case, they were stymied by the team's question about how their faith related to their work. "Does it make any difference that you are a Christian on your job?" evoked an embarrassing and embarrassed silence. Yet every person who participated indicated on their feedback sheet that they would like to meet again to talk about their work.

In midsummer of 1986, the church called its first Associate Minister, the Reverend Mr. Kenneth R. Downes. One of the criteria in his selection was his sensitivity to empowering the ministry of the laity. The church's search committee and I had deliberately chosen an associate with skills and style different from and complementary to mine. His presence as a full pastor and colleague then modeled for the congregation a way of valuing differing gifts.

The listening team's work led to the creation of a Covenant Group of ten members who spent ten months together focusing on faith and work issues. They included the three listening team members and seven others who had expressed interest. Open invitations were extended to the whole church. Both Senior and Associate Ministers met with the Covenant Group each time.

The Diaconate (the elected board responsible for spiritual life, pastoral care, and worship) of the church agreed with our assessment that our doing effective work with this one group was more important than spreading our time thinly over several. As a result, during this first year no other study groups were offered by the pastors.

Each session of the Covenant Group began with one member bringing visual reminders of her or his work and ministry and placing them on the coffee table in our meeting room. One member had us all in stitches as he pulled one item after another out of his brief-case: a stack of computer paper followed by a diaper, a Bible followed by Pepto-Bismol. Another strung a tightrope across the room to describe her work as an executive. Still another left the table empty and after a very few words set a wooden cross on it. Together we read William Diehl's *Thank God It's Monday,*[1] learned listening skills, studied the Bible, prayed and laughed and cried.

This Covenant Group experience is central to our thinking now about how we can support and challenge laity in relation to their ministries. About halfway through the year, one of the members told the group of her experience as a personnel recruiter for a large insurance company. She had been under great stress for a year before her resignation because she was told she spent too much time with each candidate. Now, a year later, she could see that she had had a significant ministry there. The conflict in values had not been clear to her at the time, and she had internalized the stress, resulting in her resignation. If only she had had a covenant group then!

In group meetings we talked about each member's life, work, and ministry. Sometimes this began from the opening time with the symbols and reminders of work and ministry. Sometimes it was more formalized. Often discussion around the Diehl book would prompt deeper sharing.

Over time, we developed some new approaches to Bible study. For one retreat, Ken and I wrote "case studies" about contemporary ministry dilemmas. Only after the group had fully explored the dilemma did we reveal that the case study was based on a biblical story. This technique made the Bible come alive for all of us in new ways. Here is one "case study" I wrote.

Meet Veronica. She and most of her family have worked at this factory for decades. They put together timing devices—do the same thing day after day, month after month, year after year. Her hands are always torn up from the work, and they never heal. Her back bothers her and her legs swell from being in one position all day.

A few years ago, somebody on the line started muttering about how the union ought to do something about "conditions." She ended up fired, and the foreman came down even heavier on them all about production. Their quota got raised and breaks got shorter, and the air conditioner's never on.

Now one of Veronica's brothers over in final assembly is starting to sound like an agitator, too. Inside, she agrees with him. They haven't had a raise in four years and things are getting worse, not better. But Veronica's got two kids to support all by herself ever since Joey freaked out with the Vietnam stuff. She can't afford to cause trouble—or even for there to be trouble. She just wants to sit tight and live through it. And she heard that the union leaders had been trying to reason with the bosses, but had gotten nowhere.

Every time someone started pushing for things to get better, they got worse instead. Veronica thinks they'd all better just shut up and be thankful they've got jobs.

[After reading the case study, invite discussion on Veronica's plight. What would ministry in the name of Jesus Christ be like for her, either to be a minister or to receive ministry? After plenty of discussion, ask the group if they can identify a Bible story that is like Veronica's. This is based on Exodus 5: 1-21.]

We used the Myers-Briggs Type Indicator to help people know themselves. That led us to identify the kinds of Bible study most helpful to different personality types. On one retreat I was leading a study of the call of Nehemiah, asking members to see how many different kinds of ministry they could find in Nehemiah 2. After just a few minutes, one member exploded with frustration. "I feel so stupid! I just can't follow this at all!" It didn't take much discussion to find that the intuitives (who enjoy conceptual styles) were right with me, but the sensates (who enjoy detail and sequencing) were all equally frustrated. So we divided into two groups along those lines to study Nehemiah, then came together and shared our insights about the text and about the process.

Incidentally, that discussion also led us to discover that (in that group at least) there were significant differences in theological emphasis between the intuitives and the sensates. The intuitives confessed that they often felt they weren't "good enough Christians" because the figure of Jesus Christ was less important for them than the Spirit or the Creator. One of the sensates came to realize why she had such a hard time with her faith: as a sensate, she needed Jesus as a concrete manifestation of God, yet as a feminist, she needed a feminine figure!

These insights from the Covenant Group experience led us to sponsor, in the winter of 1987, a conference for the whole church. We used the Myers-Briggs Type Indicator as a way to open the issues of the relation between who we are and what we do. More people than we could accommodate applied to attend.

In the fall of 1987, we gathered our second Covenant Group (by both open and specific invitation), and launched a new program, "Koinonia," to bring together old and new covenanters once a month in a time of community and learning. We soon realized that while it sounded like a good idea, it stood in the way of the second Covenant Group bonding as a group. By January we had abandoned that concept and had refocused on bimonthly meetings of the new group.

Meanwhile the first Covenant Group had decided to spread the word of the ministry of the laity. They accepted two invitations to lead workshops describing their experience, one at an ecumenical conference, "All God's People," and the other as the program at a United Church of Christ association meeting. These presentations led to other invitations, and during the year they accepted invitations to preach, lead worship, and conduct the workshop four additional times.

On the basis then of two years of experience with covenant groups, we have designed a plan for future such groups. At present the plan's rough sketch is as follows.

Covenant Group Program Design

Early Fall: Retreat
Begin with a retreat in early fall for community building, a taste of the year ahead, and work with the Myers-Briggs Type Indicator, with worship and time for meditation.

Fall: Six Sessions
These weeks concentrate on self-discovery. Gifts identification, family of origin, personal timeline, and listening skill components enable members to know one another as well as themselves. Leaders gain a lot of data from which to design future sessions. In the past we spread these components out, but have found that many adults need a time of self-discovery before they can begin to think about what their ministries might be.

Winter: Six Sessions

These weeks introduce the basic notions of ministry. Read Diehl's *Thank God It's Monday*,[2] learn some techniques for evaluating opportunities and needs in our ministry settings: understanding organizations and systems, force field analysis, institutional racism and sexism audit, stress factors. Begin to consider what is not ministry; envision a new church. Use the Center for the Ministry of the Laity's focus person technique to build on listening skills.

Spring: Five Sessions

Experience the city in a day-long or overnight immersion in Hartford to stretch members' horizons of ministry. Begin four intensive weeks of vocational discernment: What is it that God wants me to be doing with my life? Individual consultation as well as group process. We end with a retreat.

As a way of reaching the larger congregation beyond the covenant groups and those who participated in the conferences and retreats, we began in 1987 to include in Sunday worship a special vocation prayer. Each week we focused on a different occupation group. A visual reminder of the work was placed on the communion table before the cross, and a prayer was said for those who did that work. Letters were sent to all whose work would be prayed for, informing them of the date, asking for their ideas for the prayer and the visual reminders, and inviting them to be present. Here are two of the prayers:

Prayer for Electricians
(On the communion table: coils of wire and some tools)

Creator God, You are the source of all Energy and Power. We bring before You this day those who work with the power of electricity, who seek to channel, transform, and convert a dangerous energy into power for good. Guard them and keep them safe. Give them patience with tracking problems to their source, and caution in their work. And grant them a sense of ministry in their making our lives safe, in their striving for excellence, in their dealings with people. In the name of Jesus, Amen.

Prayer for Hairdressers
(On the communion table: hairdryer, wig)

Creator and creating God, we raise before You in prayer all who work as hairdressers, barbers, and beauticians, who by their creativity and skill seek to help people feel good about themselves. Be present to them and grant them patience in their many interactions with the public and co-workers. Grant them a sense of ministry in their listening to the lonely and hurting, in their ability to transform mundane interactions into meaningful relationships, in their ability to give joy and feelings of self-worth simply by their work. In the name of Jesus Christ, we pray. Amen.

Elements of all of these components will continue to be a part of our life together as we seek ways to be faithful to our vision of an empowering church.

CHAPTER II

Beyond Program: The Management System

In the midst of these years of programming, I began to reflect on the fact that virtually everything we had done on the ministry of the laity had been done outside the formal structures and systems of the church. The "structure" that had enabled them to happen was the pastoral office. Ironically, here we were trying to strengthen the ministry of the laity, and the whole program was clergy dependent!

Yet our congregation's organizational pattern had no obviously logical body to which to assign the responsibility of developing the ministry of the laity. If we did add this assignment to an existing committee, it would receive minimal attention at best, given the activity levels of all the committees. We needed to find another way, one which would ensure a comprehensive approach.

Our church has the following major parallel boards and committees:

Diaconate (responsible for spiritual and worship life and pastoral care);
Business Committee (property and finance);
Human Resources (nominating and leadership development);
Board of Religious Education (education for all ages);
Stewardship and Mission (promotion of giving and mission interpretation);
Outreach (social concerns).

The Church Council, composed entirely of chairpersons of committees, is responsible for planning and coordination.

As pastor, I began to look systematically at each of the committees and to explore how their work could be reconceived and reoriented to empower the ministries of the laity. The questions I developed at this early stage (for a course at Hartford Seminary) can be found in the Appendix. The more I worked with the subject, the more convinced I became that two moves were key: (1) every committee needed to see its job as contributing to empowerment, and (2) the Diaconate needed to claim oversight responsibility for program enhancing empowerment.

In a course on effective church management with Speed Leas, I developed a comprehensive design for an integrated management system supporting the ministry of the laity in our church. It is the design that is the substance of this chapter.

The purpose of the management system is to integrate the program, process, and structure of Colchester Federated Church into a coherent system supporting the ministry of the laity. At the start, some programmatic elements were in place, but they were discrete and disparate, not seen in relation to each other. A systems approach looks at all the components of the church's life, tests for coherence, and works at developing interrelationship. It does not simply ask that each organizational component do its part on the agenda before the church, but also that each part understand itself in dynamic relation to the whole. Interrelationship is integral to the nature of systemic work. Therefore what is described here is not only what we have done, but how we have conceptualized the work.

Program, process and organizational structure always interact to affect the identity of the congregation. In our case, we have also taken a major piece of our congregation's identity and turned it into the organizing principle for the church's life. In this way, our identity pervades our corporate being as well as our corporate doing.[3]

I have chosen to call this a management system. Of all the definitions of management I have come across, I most like the one attributed to Harold J. Leavitt, as cited by Joseph Hough: management consists of

> *Problem-solving* (planning and systematizing);
> *Implementing* (mobilizing resources to accomplish the task); and
> *Pathfinding* (envisioning and leading.)[4]

Many definitions and understandings of management focus only on the marshaling of resources to meet a need. Leavitt's inclusion of systematizing and of visionary leadership fits my experience and theological understanding of management in the local church.

In my development of the management system, I chose to focus on five major elements of the church's life identified by

Speed Leas in his course. These are: *ministry support; membership; leadership; spiritual and personal growth;* and *structure, evaluation, and process.* For each of the five, we have made assignments of responsibility and have refocused our work.

Our initial introduction of the management system took place in Diaconate meetings. For several years this board has struggled ineffectively with its role. As the church had grown from small to midsized in the early 1980s, the functions of adult education and leadership development had been assigned to new committees. The Diaconate was now responsible for oversight of worship and pastoral care and a number of housekeeping matters such as coffee hour and greeters. In significant ways, the Diaconate was dysfunctional and they knew it. Working together, the chairperson and I led the Diaconate through several months of consciousness-raising about the ministry of the laity in general. When they were ready, we asked them to read the management system paper and to talk together about the Diaconate's key role. They began to ask questions like "How do we help people understand that the church begins and ends with each person?" "How do we connect the ministry of the laity with our structure and with everything we do in the church and outside the church?" "Isn't this what church membership has always meant?"

At subsequent meetings, they focused on the structural options for their life: what would enable them to give effective leadership to the church in supporting the ministry of the laity? Clearly they had decided the Diaconate should lay claim to that role.

Eventually they decided to create a time-limited task force on the ministry of the laity accountable to the Diaconate. This task force is responsible for program planning and coordination, ministry support, and review of the systems and structures of the church in terms of their effectiveness in enhancing the ministry of the laity. Chapter Four describes their work in designing a new organizational structure for the church which will give approximately equal weight to "sending-them-out" as it does to "holding-them-here."

Ministry Support

Support for ministry takes primarily programmatic forms. Those we have adopted in Colchester have been described in Chapter One: Covenant groups; listening teams; vocation prayers and visual reminders on the communion table; retreats and conferences; sermons and worship forms.

The commissioning of laity to their ministries will be an additional step in support if the Diaconate decides to pursue that avenue. Commissioning can be supportive not only for the one being commissioned, but also for others who identify with that person in terms of ministry, friendship, and shared vision.

Another form of support that still needs attention within our system is how our church can offer financial, legal, and other concrete forms of support to its members when they choose to be whistle-blowers or take other risks for justice in relation to their workplaces or ministry settings.

In 1987, the church conducted a capital campaign to purchase a house and property situated between the meetinghouse and the parsonage. Its location was so strategic and its availability so sudden that the Business Committee recommended it be purchased, with decisions about use to be made later.

With the implementation of the management system beginning, committees and individuals began to ask how the property could be used to further the ministry of the laity. One step presently being considered is to establish a career and vocation center to offer individual counseling and group workshops both for Christians pursuing vocation and ministry issues, and for unchurched persons and those of other faiths who need career evaluation. In southeastern Connecticut, the retooling of thousands of persons who presently work in defense industry production jobs may become a serious need in the next decade. Already many persons who have had traditional trade and production jobs find their skills obsolete in an information society. Such a center can offer concrete support to supplement the emotional and spiritual support that other programs offer.

The management system by itself does not yet drive such a decision. However, the combination of change in the culture (addressed in part through program) and the system (addressed through attention to process and structure) of the church has led people to new insight and new questions. Using support for the ministries of the laity as the plumbline for our decision-making is key. When support for the ministries of the laity is a major criterion in relation to program and systemic decisions of the church, the management system is at work.

If a congregation is serious about supporting its members in discerning and living out their ministries, it must be prepared to incarnate that support in the systems of its life.

In Colchester, therefore, ministry support is not only a program function but a plumbline by which we measure the effective-

ness of our organizational work. Responsibility for both forms lies
with the Task Force on the Ministry of the Laity, the new body
created as a result of the introduction of this management system.
Responsible to the Diaconate, its function is described below in the
section on structure and evaluation. Ideally, the whole mission of
the church should be structured and focused on support for the
ministry of the laity. Its administrative work of institutional maintenance must build up the church only insofar as it serves to support
and send out ministers in the name of Jesus Christ. Yet to do that,
it must be a strong and creative institution.

Membership

Membership affiliation is an important component of a management system because it is the entry point, determining the way the
member will relate to and understand the church in future years.
The principal intervention here is the membership class and its
inclusion of major components relating to the ministry of the laity.

　　We do not rush people into membership in this church, but
invite and encourage their increasing connection with its life.
When persons are ready to affiliate formally, they participate in a
series of four membership classes. The series is offered quarterly. It
works with as few as two, but is at its best with six or more members.

　　Each session begins with time for getting acquainted, and
then deals with the following sequence of content:

　　I.　Our church's way of work: how we are organized (dis-
　　　　tribute annual report and bylaws); history (including
　　　　skeletons in the closets); understanding of membership
　　　　and its meaning. Share chart of the spiritual journey
　　　　(page 13) our church encourages.

　　II.　Gifts Identification: we use a process adapted from the
　　　　work of the Center for the Ministry of the Laity.[5] This
　　　　process involves both individual reflection and interaction
　　　　with others, and requires the entire session. Complete
　　　　interests and talents survey. Distribute "Where Do You Fit
　　　　In?" brochure about opportunities for ministry within and
　　　　outside the church. Offer up gifts in closing worship.

　　III.　Introduction to the Ministry of the Laity: using the "Is"
　　　　and "Vision" images from the Center for the Ministry of
　　　　the Laity, we ask the group to reflect together on the

Spiritual Journey Model

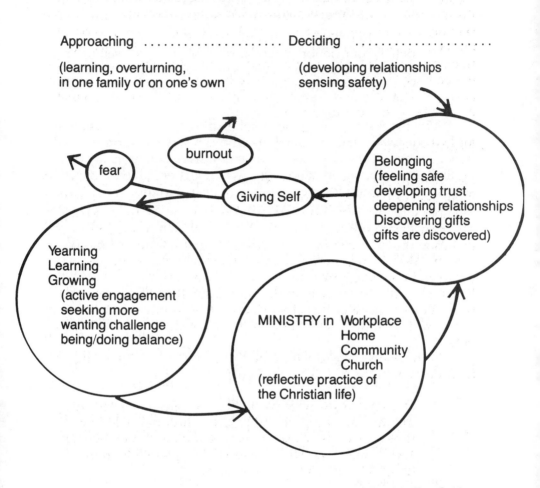

Approaching .... Deciding ....

(learning, overturning,
in one family or on one's own

(developing relationships
sensing safety)

burnout

fear

Giving Self

Belonging
(feeling safe
developing trust
deepening relationships
Discovering gifts
gifts are discovered)

Yearning
Learning
Growing
   (active engagement
   seeking more
   wanting challenge
   being/doing balance)

MINISTRY in Workplace
Home
Community
Church
(reflective practice of
the Christian life)

—Davida Foy Crabtree
June, 1987

purpose and mission of the church.[6] Taking illustrations
from the sharing they have done about their daily lives,
we weave them into the ministry ideas as we present
them, and pursue whatever avenues open up.

IV. Frank Talk about Faith and about Money: our tradition's
beliefs, our denominational relationships and setting in
Christian history; our understanding and expectations in
mission and stewardship (give out pledge cards). Closing
devotions with commissioning.

After the first session of the membership class, the pastors consult
and identify active church members who can serve as sponsors to the
new members. They are selected on the basis of commonality of age,
family status, personality, and work. When it is possible to utilize the
sponsor relationship for mentoring in ministry, we do. However, we
are still at the early stages, and need more mentors to meet the need.
Sponsorship for now is largely a means of integrating new members
into the life of a church that does not have enough small group
opportunities for friendships to develop naturally.

The assimilation of new members is problematic in this church
precisely because of the lack of small groups. The combination of the
sudden growth spurt and the leadership gap has left the church
without enough social and study groups to help new members deepen
their sense of belonging. The church positioned itself for growth in
terms of both staffing and structure because Colchester is one of the
fastest growing communities in eastern Connecticut. As a result, the
committees and boards of the church have become principal places
for the experience of ongoing community.

In this context, the program offerings in the ministry of the
laity become all the more important. They are significant commu-
nity-building and spiritual growth opportunities, and as such, they
have high appeal for newer members. However, not every person
responds to the idea of the ministry of the laity, and additional
face-to-face groups are needed in our church's life. In the next
several years, the Diaconate will need to encourage a number of
members to see the fostering of such groups as ministries which
they can offer within the church.

Leadership

As an eastern Connecticut congregation, this church's members had
for several decades been farmers, clerical and production workers,
and small business families. They have been solid, steadfast mem-

bers, thoughtful about the church and its ministry. By the 1980s, however, many younger, more professionally educated families were moving into town and there was a need for a different kind of leadership not found in the repertoire of the older, established families. Their style had been principally problem solving and reactive. The new leadership needed now was that which Bennis and Nanus refer to as anticipative and participative, a leadership that plans and engages.[7]

The growth spurt of the eighties, combined with the absence of active members between the ages of 45 and 55, meant that leadership had to be drawn from the few older members who could make the transition in leadership style, and from the newer members who are willing to take the risk of leading at a young age. The average age of committee chairpersons dropped from 54 in 1980 to 38 in 1987, and their average length of membership from 29 years to five years.

As a result the church became heavily dependent on its pastor for several years. In order to deal with that dependency and with the leadership crisis, in the 1984 planning process we created a Human Resources Committee. This new committee is responsible for gifts identification, nominations, and leadership development.

Leadership is an important aspect of the ministry of the laity. In a congregation like ours, composed of middle level workers and line workers, the experience people gain in leadership in the church enhances their ability to function well at their work. It enables them to have confidence in offering themselves for community leadership. It offers them a new sense of possibility in their families.[8] Leadership teaches leaders new ways to relate to others, whether that is in a church meeting, at home, in a civic organization, or at work.

At Colchester Federated Church, the Human Resources Committee has developed a job description for every board and committee position.[9] When members are asked to serve in positions in the life of the church, the committee gives them a copy of the appropriate job description, and asks them to consider the invitation for several days before giving an answer. At the beginning of each new leadership year, a training program is offered to all continuing and new committee members and leaders. Special leadership development events are given for chairpersons, and orientation sessions are held for the new members on each committee. Exit interviews are conducted with outgoing leaders. New chairpersons are urged to meet with old chairpersons before the first meeting of their administration. A specific person is charged with the responsibility of encouraging and organizing our members' participation in denominational and ecumenical workshops which broaden their horizons and give them new skills.

The booklet "Where Do You Fit In?" was developed by the Human Resources Committee, and is used with all members, old and new, throughout the year. While this resource focuses primarily on volunteer ministries within the life of the church, it does also point to the fact that all Christians are called to be in ministry throughout all their lives.

The adoption of the ministry of the laity as a plumbline in our church's life has also caused another major change in our work: a new emphasis on gifts identification for a person's whole life. In membership class, in committee meetings, in program groups, when we do gifts identification now, it is done as a service to the person, not just as a self-serving talent hunt on the part of the church. We learn to consult, coach, and collaborate with each other in strengthening people instead of merely the institution.

One of the goals of this management system has been to develop an explicitly Christian leadership for Colchester Federated Church. We can take all the best human development tools from the corporate and nonprofit worlds, but if our members are not equipped to reflect on their lives, their ministries, and their leadership from a Christian perspective, then we have only reinforced the notion of the church as a membership club or a community organization.

Therefore this goal must and does influence the way Human Resources undertakes its leadership development work. However, it is important to note that the covenant groups especially, and other programs in the ministry of the laity as well, foster theological reflection in considerable depth. While they have focused on ministry in the workplace, members quickly grasp the ways in which that reflection carries over into their lives in the church.

The best example of covenant group reflection linking workplace and church came as the group discussed a chapter of *Thank God It's Monday*[10] on the concept of principalities and powers. For most of the group, employers were not the only principalities and powers in their lives. The church ran a close second. Since these were people deeply committed to the church's life, it was easy for that commitment to become a demanding, sometimes almost demonic, force in their lives. In reflecting on that reality, new insights were gained about the nature of the church and ministry, about New Testament understandings of principalities and powers, and about work ethic and works righteousness. Certainly, then, the various programmatic components also serve to strengthen the leadership development aspect of the system.

One cannot discuss leadership in the local church without mentioning the clergy. Throughout the life of this program, I have attempted to observe myself as well as the church. There are many changes that the implementation of this management system has in store for me as pastor. The next chapter lays out a theology of ministry which focuses on creation, incarnation and empowerment. This theological stance necessarily leads to constant change in one's style and skills in relation to the needs of the church.

In particular, the introduction of major changes in leadership development and empowerment means functional changes in my leadership style. A church that has been dependent on me is coming of age; I need to step back. A program that has grown from my commitment has come to be owned by the congregation; I need to let go. A system I have designed has begun to be implemented; I need to empower. More steps yet need to be taken; I need to envision and to lead. I have had to work hard at expanding my repertoire of leadership skills and styles.

As we send people out as ministers in and to the world, they have less time and energy for ministry within the institutional church. So perhaps the greatest challenge has been to ensure that I affirm ministries beyond the institution even when it means that some of *my* hopes and dreams for my workplace will take longer to achieve.

Spiritual and Personal Growth

In relation to the ministry of the laity, there are three aspects of spiritual and personal growth that need to be considered: worship life, educational program, and personal support.

Worship Life: Sunday worship is prime time for nurturing the vital connection between faith and life, especially between work and ministry. We do not usually think of worship in relation to the development of a management system, yet it is the primary identity time for the local church. We build community, form a corporate identity, and establish a common language there. Worship must be understood not solely as a program of the church, but as the determining factor in creating an ethos of receptivity, in positioning the church in a viable niche in the community, in creating both identity and that sense of belonging essential to a vital organization. Unlike most social organizations, the church has a collective experience every week. The corporate personality of the particular congregation, its life-style and values are all evident when it gathers for worship.

Because most people think of Sunday worship when they think of "church," it is critically important that we develop ways of bridging the gap between faith and work during our worship time. If we use only educational events to bridge it, people will still feel that there is a gap in their lives. If we are able to integrate life and work issues with worship, and do so with authenticity and power, the gap can be minimized.

The management system assigns worship responsibilities to the Diaconate with the Senior Minister. This is a church which has not had lay readers. Until the advent of the ministry of the laity emphasis, only one Sunday a year included lay participation and preaching. Now we have as many as five such Sundays annually. Yet it is still the norm that clergy lead all the worship on a given Sunday morning.

There is both blessing and curse in that. On the one hand, because we have not made mini-clergy out of the laity, "ministry of the laity" is not perceived here to mean only ministry within the church.[11] On the other hand, the absence of lay leadership means that worship may not be perceived as the work of the people.

The issues the Diaconate will address under the new system include lay leadership of worship, worship forms that enhance the connection between faith and work, and the commissioning of laity to their ministries. As we look at worship through the lens of concern for the ministries of the laity in their workplaces, we will confront profound issues related to Word and sacrament, ordination, and vocation. We will have to address the relationship between baptism and ministry; the relation of baptism to ordination; the role and responsibility of the ordained in this new understanding of church.

Traditionally the church has commissioned educators, missionaries, and leaders to their work within the church. It has not historically conducted commissioning services for laity who have felt called to other kinds of work. In our experience, as a person develops the capacity for critical reflection on his or her life work, very often he or she begins to be clear about God's calling. In some cases, a person may "know" that God has called her to a specific job, such as teaching math to junior high school students. In other cases, a person may come to identify his ministry in more general terms (a ministry of peacemaking), but with equal certainty of God's calling.

In the churches' traditions, we have liturgies for many passages of life: baptism, confirmation, marriage, death. Yet when an adult comes to a new conviction (or wants to affirm a lifelong awareness) of God's will for his or her use of the life that God has given, we have nothing to offer. This management system, with its attention to worship that integrates faith and work/ministry, raises the issue of commissioning.

Educational Program: Education for persons of all ages is important to the ministry of the laity. The Board of Religious Education is responsible to address the issue of how to teach the ministry of all God's people to children, youth, and adults. Because the Diaconate's responsibility for spirituality overlaps with adult education, the two boards coordinate their work with each other.

Adult education is a frontier for renewed ministry in the local church, especially with baby boomers returning to the church. Our position in Colchester has been strategic for this renewal. As we grow, we are able to offer more programs tailored to particular constituencies. This growth parallels the arrival in town of hundreds of new young families. There is no other mainline Protestant church of our size within seventeen miles, and in Colchester the other choices are Bible Baptist, Assembly of God, Roman Catholic, a small continuing Congregationalist church, and the Jewish synagogue. We are well positioned, having established a viable niche and a clear identity.

Now we are using our position and the happenstance of demographics to create a new understanding of the church as new people affiliate. When people enter a new environment they are most open to change. They expect things to be different. Worship and adult education (including the membership class as well as after-worship educational forums and evening study groups) are entry points for people, and must be used strategically in any management system.

In this system, the Diaconate and its Task Force on the Ministry of the Laity described below periodically review the effectiveness with which we are utilizing all the many occasions for teaching about the ministry of all God's people. In every church these include classes and study groups, but also committee meetings, choir practice and pastoral counseling sessions.

Personal Support: Much of the role of the church in people's lives is that of providing personal support. Through the cultivation of a vital faith, the offering of a community of caring, and the provision of pastoral care, the individual is strengthened for daily life. Or at least that is the assumption.

In truth, many people do not experience the church that way. They find their life vis-a-vis the church filled with doubt, conflicting feelings, loneliness, and a fear of dependency. For some, the church becomes another principality and power in their lives. It does not have to be that way, but that is the way it is for far too many.

Support for individuals does not have to be dependent on the clergy exerting a professionalized pastoral care. Most people simply need friends, others who listen and care. Yet many, perhaps most, people do not know how to be friends.

In relation to the ministry of the laity, our teaching each other the language and skills of compassion, active listening, and a willingness to share our own vulnerability has begun to transform the experience known as "church." It has a positive effect on home and family relationships, work lives, and responsiveness to the needs of others in the community. Members relate experiences of listening and hearing their spouses and coworkers in new ways. They begin, for instance, to hear the expression of needs not as complaints but as opportunities for ministry. Such work begins to decrease the unhealthy dependency of individuals on the pastors, and contributes also to the reduction of institutional dependency on clergy.

Personal support is a function of belonging. As such it is not solely comprised of one-to-one relationships, but also group identity and support. This is a major reason for the development of face-to-face groups in the life of a lively church—not simply because they help a church hold on to members, but because the group life contributes to the spiritual and personal growth of the members. Therefore in this management system, all of our discussions and decisions about small groups, committee life and leadership development feed into the personal support component. In particular, the nurturing of maintenance as well as task agendas in committees takes on new meaning. It is important not simply because it results in better productivity, but also because it contributes to spiritual and personal growth, to bonding and belonging.

In this system, personal support oversight is the responsibility of the Diaconate. They are mandated to develop the nurturing opportunities that the church so often lacks in natural and created supports for friendship building. The Human Resources Committee is charged with ensuring that leaders understand the importance of committees as communities, and the way the balance of task and maintenance functions contribute to wholistic experiences in the faith community.

Structure

The introduction of any planned change in an organization is risky business. Precisely because we are dealing with an institution, we find ourselves up against a weighted status quo. It is a major challenge to move the organization from simply being receptive to new program to reordering its life around a new concept.

Yet if we do not intervene in the structural and systemic life of the institution, the change never takes root. It loses its opportunity to transform the institution as well as the persons who make up the institution.

Therefore our management system does not simply identify the points in the organization's existing life that need to be coordinated or enhanced. Rather, it goes on to provide for a body within the organization that will review and evaluate the effectiveness of both organizational structure and program on the basis of their contribution to the support of the ministry of the laity.

The Diaconate debated a number of alternative structures to take on responsibility for the ministry of the laity. They saw that its assignment to a specific body was imperative for success in the conversion of the institution. The alternatives discussed included the Diaconate itself; the Church Council; the creation of a new, separate, permanent board or committee; the appointment of a separate board for three years only; and finally the appointment of a task force subsidiary to the Diaconate for a period of a year or more as needed.

They chose this last option in large part because they understand the ministry of the laity as a Diaconate function, yet also because they knew they could not take it all on at once. Under this plan, the following are the responsibility assignments:

Diaconate:
Membership process and program
Worship and commissioning
Personal support and pastoral care

Task Force on the Ministry of the Laity:
Program planning and coordination
Ministry support
Systemic review and structural evaluation

Human Resources:
Gifts identification
Leadership nomination and development

Religious Education:
Educational program for all ages

It was originally conceived that when the Task Force completed its review of the work of each board and committee in the church and had assessed the most effective way for the church's energy to be harnessed for supporting the ministry of the laity, then all of its functions would be transferred to the Diaconate. However, the task force chose to develop an entirely new organizational structure for the church. (See Chapter Four.)

Having the Diaconate concentrate on the ministry of the laity functions that are most like its traditional responsibilities gives them time and opportunity to reach a deeper understanding of the implications of their new perspective for all of their work. The membership growth and assimilation issues alone are worth an entire year's work. So is commissioning. It is for these reasons that the Diaconate saw the wisdom of appointing a short term task force to take on some of the other functions and keep the momentum going.

The agenda before the task force continues to be hefty. Its main job has been to serve as an intervention in the church's organization in order to consolidate the developments of the past several years and to ensure that the ministry of the laity does not degenerate into a purely programmatic issue, but includes attention to systemic and structural questions. They are a diverse and committed group, with a great breadth and depth of experience. They have needed to acquaint themselves with the work of all the committees in the church and to adopt a critical perspective on the way we are organized. They have had to develop a common language and a common understanding of the way systems work. One of their achievements has been the structural design described in chapter four.

Evaluation

Evaluation has been conducted in relation to every program throughout these years. At the end of each component, we have had the members evaluate their experience, and the results have been used in designing succeeding programs. Continuing evaluation of program is one of the agendas for the task force. It not only conducts evaluation, but seeks ways to build ongoing evaluation into the way we work. Since there are no proven systems for the shepherding of the ministry of the laity in a local congregation, our self-evaluation at every point is imperative. By doing so, we will be able to strengthen our own life and contribute to the larger movement.

Not everyone in the church is ready for full participation in the movement for the ministry of the laity. Throughout these years, we have tried not to create an elite nor to exclude or alienate those who are at a other points in their spiritual journeys. The Covenant Groups themselves have been sensitive to this issue and have sought actively to interpret their presence to the church in an open way. Having members from different age and social groups in the church has helped. Offering other opportunities to connect to the ministry of the laity program (retreats, conferences, listening teams) has honored the different levels of commitment. The pastors have been disciplined in their commitment to keep the process open to all.

· Evaluation of progress must also include the large constituency of the church that chooses not to participate directly in program. The Diaconate and the task force will need to have some understanding of adult faith development and its relation to human growth and need. Making the future structure and program non-threatening and yet challenging, inviting rather than alienating, is a key to their success over the long term.

We have tried a number of different ways of evaluating the overall emphasis. All of them have been complicated by the fact that we did not know we were doing significant work until fairly far along in the process. As a result, we do not have any baseline information.

If we had surveyed members seven years ago about, for instance, their attitudes toward the connection between faith and daily life, we could survey them again and test for growth.

We did invite a consultant to interview a small cross-section of members in the spring of 1988 to ascertain the impact of the covenant groups on the life of the church, the effectiveness of my pastoral leadership, and the level of understanding of the basic ideas of the management system.

Her findings affirmed the covenant groups as a program strategy. Group members felt it had enriched their work and personal lives, deepened their spirituality and given them a real sense of ministry. Those outside the groups had gotten the message that the groups were good experiences, but did not feel less a part of the church themselves.

She also found that without exception the laity saw my strong leadership on the issue as a key ingredient. One person said, "You need the energy and enthusiasm of someone who will do the pushing for a while."

Those interviewed saw the management system as a way to ensure the continuation of the emphasis on the ministry of the laity beyond my tenure as pastor and beyond the tenure of the current lay leadership.

In a completely different approach to evaluation, we looked at the process of introducing the management system. We were greatly helped by Jackson W. Carroll's unpublished paper, "Some Notes on Planned Social Change." At the end of that paper, he identifies twenty-six factors facilitating the acceptance of planned change.[12] We applied these factors to the management system process as a way of assessing how effective we had been in introducing it. The complete list of factors is in the Appendix. The following is a summary of the strengths and weaknesses of the process we used. The numbers in brackets after each item refer to the factor in Carroll's paper which is applied in that item.

Strengths:

1. Considerable time was spent making the connection between Christian normative values and the program before any notion of systemic change was introduced. [4.1 (1)]

2. We addressed not only the culture of the organization, but the structure as well. [4.1 (2)]

3. The project enhances the autonomy of members; it reduces reliance on the authority of clergy and makes the laity the authorities on their own ministries. [4.1 (3), 4.2 (2)]

4. It provides a new and interesting experience, and responds to emotional, intellectual, and spiritual felt needs. [4.1 (6)]

5. The program and process was introduced over a long period of time. [4.1 (8)]

6. Time was taken to ensure understanding by all members of the Diaconate. [4.1 (9)]

7. We adopted a direction that is open and amenable to change if needed. It does not force the abandoning of current practice all at once. [4.1 (11), (12)]

8. Covenant group members and Diaconate came to a high degree of ownership of vision, strategy, and process. [4.2 (1)]

9. Full support of top leaders, clergy, and lay was built. [4.2 (3)]

10. Accommodations were made to gain support of gatekeepers. [4.2 (4)]

11. I limited my use of power to envisioning, initial program development, and proposal of structure. [4.3 (1), (3)]

12. By using the management system paper with the Diaconate, clear diagnosis, goals, guidelines, accountability, and proposals for evaluation were present. [4.3 (2), (5), (7)]

13. The early, visible success of the first Covenant Group gave impetus to the entire effort. [4.3 (8)]

14. Formative feedback has been a part of every aspect of the project, both by those involved and by others in the congregation. [4.3 (9)]

15. The establishment of the task force (and later assignment of the role to Diaconate or some other body) makes for clear accountability for implementation of systemic changes. [4.3 (10)]

Weaknesses:

1. The program and system are profoundly compatible with Christian values and norms, but in conflict with operating norms of churches. [4.1 (1)]

2. The changes can easily be perceived as adding to participants' burdens. [4.1 (5)]

3. The proposed changes pervade the entire system of the church, leaving nothing untouched. [4.1 (7)]

4. The innovation is not simple and easy to understand. [4.1 (9)]

5. We don't know any examples of other similar systems that have successfully adopted this change. [4.1 (10)]

6. The central message of the project is incompatible with existing organizational arrangements; pervasive restructuring was needed. [4.2 (4)]

7. We did not succeed in permanently altering the structure and process of the church so as to institutionalize change. It is still in process. [4.3 (10)]

Many of these are weaknesses in that they make change more difficult to introduce into the church system, but strengths in that they contribute to a wholistic approach. For instance, weaknesses number one and three contribute to the overall strength of the management system. Yet both have made implementation difficult. The fact that the notion of the ministry of the laity is deeply rooted in scripture and the church's teachings does not diminish the difficulty of overcoming years of antithetical traditional practice.

One of the strengths of this project is also the reason it is difficult to evaluate: it constitutes the foundation of an ongoing intervention in a local church system. As identified earlier, local churches are organized to serve their own institutional ends. Administrative committees predominate. Even those committees that focus on mission and ministry do so vis–a–vis the corporate entity of the church and not to send the members out in their own ministries. The full weight of Christian institutional history stands over against this effort to turn one mainline Protestant church into a sending-them-out system rather than a holding-them-here system.

So these have been to date the components of our management system: membership, leadership, spiritual, and personal growth, ministry support, and structure and evaluation. I have described the history of the idea in our congregation, the process by which we have come to this point, and the culmination of this project in the initial stages of implementation of the management system. As with any comprehensive intervention in an organization, the full fruits will be borne in years to come.

CHAPTER III

Creation, Incarnation, Empowerment

By now the reader is probably wondering what the theological basis for this work is. This chapter focuses attention on three overarching themes which inform a ministry that takes laity and the church seriously: Creation, Incarnation, and Empowerment.

For me, theology is lived, not just thought. Therefore it is always to some degree autobiographical. Yet it is also rooted in the broad sweep of Christian history, in the thousands of years of expectations inherited in the present age.

It is also the case that often theology is one thing, practice another. These pages describe an operational theology that has been shaped profoundly by Colchester Federated Church and our life together in ministry. Most theologies are shaped more by what the theologian is fighting against than by any great cohesive vision, despite our wanting it to be otherwise. Self-consciousness about the points of struggle and "rough edges" of life in ministry is, with personal autobiography and Christian tradition, a component of theologizing.

When I first came to Colchester, I experienced this church more as a membership club or social organization than a Christian church. It was clearly a club filled with people who were a delight to be with, and I was glad I was here. Yet I frequently wondered whether it would be possible to help them be a church, given the entrenched traditions and assumptions, and given the low self-image in which the people viewed themselves and their church. We have come a long way since then, both congregation and pastor.

For me, the three principles which form the core of my theology of ministry are the three identified above: Creation, Incarnation, and Empowerment.

These form the basis of my understanding of ministry, sacrament, and institution. They undergird my convictions about my role as pastor, about the layperson's role as minister, and about the church's role in mission to the world.

Creation

In the act of creation, God gave rise to a world of good and laid upon humanity full responsibility for that world. At the same moment, God revealed Godself as Creator, affirmed that humanity is created in God's image, and expressed a divine intention for our creativity.

From this foundational affirmation arise a number of theological motifs in my ministry.

The World and Life Are Good

About two years after my arrival in Colchester, an old woodsman named Charlie Kramer came to church one Sunday when we were in the midst of reading a litany. All eyes focused on him at once, voices faltered, the liturgy was broken (yet also strikingly fulfilled). As someone said to me later, "No one has ever been able to get Charlie to come to church!" When this was said to me again after Charlie had been in church for five successive weeks, I suggested that they ask him why he came, since I wanted to know too. They reported back that he had said, "All those other preachers on TV and radio and even here all these years have threatened us with hell. This little lady tempts us with heaven, and that's the way it should be."

From my conviction that God's creation is good flows a preaching and a pastoring that focuses on what Matthew Fox has called our original blessing.[13] In my grandmother's words, "You catch more flies with honey than you do with vinegar." I am more oriented toward God's goodness than I am toward our sin. I gain my energy from, and give my energy to, the wonders of life rather than our failings as human beings.

When a word needs to be spoken over against some form of sin or injustice, I do speak it. The identifying of evil in our world is a prophetic act of creativity, always pointing to God's creation and God's acts in history as signs of God's intent for our life together. Still, I believe that the primary word from God is a word of blessing, not a word of curse.

When in the church we share the sacraments of baptism and communion, we are sharing in the richness of God's creation. Baptism is a time of turning (or being turned, in infant baptism) toward God's goodness, of being grafted onto the family of God. It is a washing with hope more than a cleansing from sin. Communion is a participation in the richness of God's good dominion. It is a mystical oneness with all creation at the same time that it is specifically a oneness with Jesus Christ and the church of all time. The waters, grains, and fruits of the earth are signs to us of God's blessing of our community.

We Are Stewards of Creation

Responsibility and intentionality are key words for me. In creation, God has given us dominion over all the earth. The consequences of that responsibility are far-reaching.

Being a steward of creation is not just being a trustee for the natural world. It is exercising a care for all the world in all we do. Human society and all its ancillaries are also a part of creation. As a pastor, one of my prime responsibilities is to teach and preach in such a way that all God's people come to understand that their primary vocation is as stewards of creation. All that we do either contributes to God's ongoing Creation or undermines it, either promotes the blessing or turns it into curse.

We Are Created in God's Image

Fifteen years ago, five of us were crammed into a small Toyota in New York City, heading for a meeting of our denominational task force on women. As we rounded a corner and hurtled onto the West Side Highway, I suggested that the theme for our first national meeting of women be "Created in God's Image." The driver of the car, now a prominent executive and therefore nameless, almost lost us all in the river. "How could we ever do that? It's so arrogant!" came the response.

Yet I continue to believe that it is only as both women and men fully come to understand their creation in God's image that our world can be freed of its alienation from God. To acknowledge our creation in God's image is an act of humility, not arrogance. It affirms our source and identity. It makes us question in which image of God we are created. It brings us face to face with the sinful arrogance of the assumptions on which we have operated for the last several thousand years.

We are—all of us—created in God's image. Therefore we are persons of worth. Therefore we share in dominion, both male and female. Therefore we are called to creativity, as the God in whose image we are created is the Creator.

In the church, the primary rite of admission and acceptance is
baptism, a ritual which is available to both male and female. In the
moment of baptism we affirm, whether we state it or not, that all are
called alike to the ministries of creativity, stewardship, and grace.

In theology of ministry, the divine intentionality for our
creativity is pivotal. If ministry is seen only as the passing on of
the tradition, it stultifies the creativity to which I believe God
calls us. Yet it is also true that if ministry is always only the creating of the new, then it becomes thin and loses the richness of all
that has gone before. The tension between the old and the new
must be elastic, creative, and dynamic if Christian ministry is to be
fruitful.

I am aware that not many begin with creation in speaking of
ministry. Yet it was the wonder of the natural world that first interested me in faith. As a child I was always bringing home bugs,
snakes, flowers, rocks, even dead fish. My parents encouraged my
questions and kept a sense of humor about it all. I looked around
me and saw the hand of God in the beauty and complexity of the
natural world. Gradually I came to affirm our human partnership
with God in ongoing creation and to understand that we are all
called to ministry.

Incarnation

The incarnation of God in Jesus Christ teaches us that our life is
not alien to God, but known intimately and fully in its joy and
pain. Jesus' life and ministry, death, and resurrection carry within
them the meaning of our lives and our life.

The church is the Body of Christ in the world, continuing to
live out the incarnation, ministry, death and resurrection of the
Christ in every time and place. As such the church is called to
embody [em-body, structure, incarnate] Christ's ministry. We must
not flinch when called upon to die, and must be catalysts for the
resurrection in our day.

It is the whole church that is the Body of Christ, the church at
worship and the church at work, the church gathered and the
church scattered. Christ's ministry continues through all the people,
and not only when they are together in one place "in" what we
call the church, but also when they are spread forth over the face
of the earth living as disciples and ministers of Jesus Christ.

Incarnation is inseparable from creation. In the incarnation,
God continued to create. In our attempts to incarnate the presence
of God in our day, we continue to create.

An incarnational theology of ministry puts great weight on community, structure, and purpose because these are the ways we embody the ministry of Christ in our day.

Community

It is as we understand our community of faith as the Body of Christ that its life begins to take on meaning beyond that of a membership club. Being the Body of Christ means that we are intentional, missional, and willing to give up our whole life. It means that we are corporate, bodying forth what we believe. It means that how we live together is most important because our body is a visible sign to the world.

The Pauline letters are full of references to the parts of the body, to the differing gifts which God has given us (Romans 12). A theology of ministry founded on the Incarnation is rooted in community because it is only as we are community that we are the Body. In that corpus called the church, if we reflect theologically from the vantage point of the Body of Christ, every member is equally valued and equally needed, and can be equally in ministry.

The Body of Christ known as the church is transformative for human life because in the name of Jesus Christ it sets persons in relation to one another in a grace-filled context, calls them to be more than they are, and empowers them to risk. It is transformative because it embodies in its way of being, ever so haltingly, the real presence of Jesus Christ. It is transformative because it does not exist for itself, but for the world.

In ministry, we are about the building up of the Body of Christ, not for its own sake, but for the world's. Christ came to serve. We are here to serve. As the church is servant to the world, seeking its transformation and restoration, so the ordained minister is servant to the church. The servant community is the essential identity of the Christian church as the Body of Christ.

Structure

God gave form to God's caring for the world in the incarnation. So are we called to give form to our caring for the world.

Therefore one consequence of a theology of ministry rooted in the incarnation is careful attention to structures for mission and ministry. If we live and minister by an incarnational theology, we cannot reduce our ministry solely to individualistic foci. We recognize that sin can take institutional and systemic forms as well as personal, that injustice is as real as prejudice, that individual salvation is not sufficient for our world's reality. We affirm that attention to organizational matters in the local church's life can be as life-giving to persons as attention to pastoral care. An incarnational theology encourages us to teach and preach with care for the total matrix in which all God's people live out their lives, and with recognition of their being caught in the complex web of conflicting loyalties in contemporary life.

The Body of Christ is not a spiritualized cloud of a dream, but a tough, fleshy reality. It lives in the midst of compromise and politics, lives by our willingness to enflesh the gospel in structures for its mission and ministry. An incarnational theology of ministry gives no credence to ministry that pays no attention to structures and politics and institutions. It holds such ministries as heretical.

Purpose

The Body of Christ cannot simply exist. If it does, it is not the Body of the Christ whom God sent out of love for the world (John 3:16). If the church is the Body of Christ, then it has a purpose, the same purpose as Jesus Christ's: to transform and restore the world to its original harmony with God.

The Body of Christ is called upon to utilize all the human material and spiritual resources it has at its disposal to accomplish this purpose. None can be set aside. All the differing gifts are necessary.

I am sure that my conviction about the value and importance of every person to the ministry and mission of the church stems not only from my creation and incarnation centered theology, but also from my own experience as one whose gifts were nearly rejected by the church. My struggle as a woman in ministry has shaped my consciousness of the gifts of all. It is no mere happenstance that I am committing so many of my personal resources to the ministry of the laity. Once one's eyes have been opened, they do not close again easily.

So the gifts of all are necessary to the mission of the Body of Christ. In our reflection on Creation, we have seen that both men and women are included in the image and dominion of God. Here in our reflection on Incarnation, we see that both clergy and laity are fully part of the Body of Christ, with differing gifts equally valued.

In the Body of Christ, all are baptized. No distinction is made between men and women, or those who will someday be clergy

and those who will continue as laity. Baptism is the central rite of
the church. All others are given to sustain and build up the Body
that is created by the administration of this sacrament. In this view,
communion was instituted by Jesus to sustain baptized believers in
their ministries after his death and resurrection. Ordination is given
as a means to equip the whole church to live out their baptismal
vows. Even worship has the principal purpose of building up the
Body in community, faith, and mission.

If the purpose of this Body of baptized believers is the transformation of the world, then the work and ministry of every person
every moment of every day is important. If it is the world we are
concerned about, and not just the upbuilding of the institution we
know as church, then the laity are more important than the clergy.
The laity, after all, are the ones who move in and out of the halls
of power and the back alleys of powerlessness.

An incarnational theology of ministry affirms that the Body of
Christ is at work wherever its members are at work. While I believe we are called to be at work self-consciously and intentionally
as the Body of Christ in all those places, I also believe that Christ
works through us even when that is not the case. In *Mutual Ministry,* James Fenhagen comments, "The New Testament is quite clear
about this. Ministry is an act undertaken in the name of Christ...
Ministry is an act performed in his name. Therefore, it is not
something we do solely on our own, but something Christ does in
us, through us, and with us."[14]

Finally, if we are to be truly the Body of Christ, we must
always be prepared to risk crucifixion and death. We must, as a
corporate entity, be clear about where we draw the lines for our
integrity. We must never cooperate with injustice, but always stand
for justice, even when that means suffering.

Of all aspects of an incarnational theology of ministry, this is the
one that is the hardest to live and to teach. Very few want to hear it,
and very few therefore ever understand it. Yet without this understanding, the theology is vapid. If the church does not develop
autonomy in its relation to the world, it cannot be the Body of Christ.

Empowerment

The role of the ordained minister takes its image from Christ the
servant. One important job description is set forth in Ephesians 4:12:

> to equip the saints for the work of ministry, for building up
> the body of Christ.

And a job description for all the people of God is found in the
continuation of that same passage, Ephesians 4:13-16:

> until we all attain to the unity of the faith and of the knowl-
> edge of the Son of God, to mature humanity, to the measure
> of the stature of the fullness of Christ; so that we may no
> longer be children, tossed to and fro and carried about with
> every wind of doctrine, by human cunning, by craftiness in
> deceitful wiles. Rather, speaking the truth in love, we are to
> grow up in every way into Christ who is the head, into Christ,
> from whom the whole body, joined and knit together by
> every joint with which it is supplied, when each part is work-
> ing properly, makes bodily growth and upbuilds itself in love.
> [RSV, adapted by DFC]

The sheer volume of words in the difference of those two job
descriptions carries a message. The task of the ordained is simple
and straightforward: "to equip the saints for the work of ministry,
for building up the body of Christ." The task of the whole people
of God is far from simple, however. In this passage,it seems oriented toward building up itself. Yet the image Paul uses is the
Body of Christ, and Christ, as we have seen, lived for the world.

The task of the ordained clergy is to enable the church to
build itself up into a self-consciously Christian community set free
to ministries of reconciliation and transformation in the world. (*In
Ministry as Reflective Practice,* I found the references to a community of meaning, belonging, and empowerment especially helpful.
The foregoing statement of the task of the ordained is intended to
encompass those dimensions.[15]) Each community will have different gifts, capacities, and opportunities for such ministries, just as
individuals do. Therefore the shape of those ministries will differ
from place to place. The task of the clergy is to enable the particular community of faith to discover its unique vocation by careful
attention to identity, context, process, program, and structure.

My job as ordained leader is not to do the equipping of the
individuals (though in some cases I must), but to build up the
community in such a way that the community empowers itself by
its living as the Body of Christ, by its explicit acts of training and
teaching.

So we see that "equipping the saints" must not be interpreted
only in reference to individuals, but also in reference to the community. In this theological motif of empowerment the motifs of
creation and incarnation come to fruition. Responsibility for the

stewardship of the world, development of our capacities for creativity, incarnating Christ's work in ours, embodying our faith in structures of reconciliation in both church and world—all these feed into the theological development of a ministry of empowerment.

A theology of individual salvation would feed one kind of empowerment. This theology of creation and incarnation feeds an empowerment of community, which in turn nurtures and drives the empowerment both of individuals in their ministries in the world and of the faith community in its mission in the world. Community and individual are in dynamic tension. Both are sources of creativity, incarnation, and empowerment, and both are the loci of God's action.

The Ephesians text quoted above emphasizes the role of the faith community. It is corporately directed, not individually. Drawing together my understanding of creation, incarnation, and empowerment, then, it is clear that the role of the ordained minister is to build community in such a way that it embodies and empowers the mission and ministry of all God's people in and to the world. I am not the empowerer. The Holy Spirit, which infuses the Body of Christ with vitality and power, does the empowering of the faith community. I am charged to equip the saints (plural, not "each saint") so that the community may be built up and their ministries discovered, sustained, and strengthened. The Spirit works in and through the faith community, and therefore sometimes in and through me.

Part of my responsibility as an ordained person in the role of equipping the saints is to clarify and interpret the structures and systems which shape the life of the community of faith. I do not do it alone, but always (as with everything in ministry) in the midst of that community. Yet I do bear a primary responsibility for holding those structures and systems up against the light of the tradition and the window of contemporary experience and knowledge so that the particular community's unique mission may be carried out without hindrance (read: empowered).

Based in this theological perspective, I hold to a conviction that the ordained are not the "set apart" ones. At baptism, we are all set apart. At ordination some are set in the midst of those who are set apart, set in the midst to serve and equip the Body of Christ for ministry.

In this understanding, pastoral care, worship leadership, celebration of the sacraments, and administration of organizational life are functions contributing to the empowerment of the community of faith for its ministries as the Body of Christ.

Those who are ordained do bear responsibility for pastoral care. Yet it is not the final definition of clergy responsibility. Pastoral care and leadership must take many forms other than those implied by either the traditional cure of souls or the contemporary therapeutic model. Counseling, befriending, nurturing belonging, encouraging personal growth and lifetime learning, developing viable structures for the organizational life of the church are all oriented toward enabling the person and the community of faith more fully to live as ministers of Jesus Christ.

Those who are ordained do bear responsibility for worship and the celebration of the sacraments. Yet worship is an act of the whole people of God, drawn together in joy to celebrate and affirm their oneness with Christ and all creation, their assent to God's sovereignty in their lives, and their shared life as the Body of Christ. It is a time of renewal and strengthening and as such it must reflect the truth of their lives. It is a time of blessing and commissioning, of sending forth into ministry, and as such it must reflect the powers with which they must contend. It is a time of leading and empowering, and as such it must reflect the heights and depths of which they are capable and to which they are drawn.

Likewise we bear responsibility for administering the organizational life of the church. When clergy complain about their administrative loads, it usually means they operate out of a different theological base than I do. Management can be one of the most creative, incarnational, and empowering forms of ministry the local church offers. It all depends how one does it, and how one understands the goal. In this understanding, administrative management is highly valued when it builds up the community as a vital center for ministry. Every act of management must be scrutinized for its contribution to the accomplishment of this intent. When it is just perpetuating the institution or tinkering with structures, then it is unfruitful and to be spurned.

So Creation, Incarnation, and Empowerment are woven together into a single fabric forming a theology of ministry which mandates support for laity in their ministries and insists that the church take seriously its own structures and systems as incarnations of its beliefs.

CHAPTER IV

A Structure for the Church's Mission

If the task of the church is to empower its members for ministry, then the church needs to be structured organizationally to reflect that task. We need to create, incarnate, and empower our theological beliefs in the way we organize ourselves.

At Colchester we have only begun to define the new structure I will outline here. It is in its earliest stages, and has not yet been introduced to the congregation. The Diaconate and the Church Council have seen the design and have begun to discuss its advantages and disadvantages. They have projected a one year timeline for introducing the basic ideas and implications to the rest of the church. It is important to note that if and when a new structure is put into place, much of our work on the management system will need to be reevaluated and recast. However, systems work is never done, for even the most minor adjustment shifts interaction throughout the system and requires reevaluation.

As you read, please bear in mind that this is only conceptual at this point. It has not been tested either by the wisdom of the larger congregation or by actual implementation. Yet I share it here because it may help the reader understand more fully our critique of present local church structures.

Form must follow function. When our task force on the ministry of the laity met to spend a day exploring possible designs for our future structure, this was our cardinal principle. We began by writing a succinct mission statement (as one must do for any effective planning task). Since our church was already fairly clear about its mission (or at least the task force was!), this part of the process was easy. Here is the statement we developed:

Colchester Federated Church: empowering members for ministries in workplace, home, church, and community.

Having identified our function, we then began to work at the form that could incarnate it. We knew that we wanted to end up with a structure that would give equal time, energy, and resources to sending people out in ministry as it does to keeping the institutional base strong. The mission statement gave us a clear identification of four ministries. We then worked at defining four ministries that would enable us to maintain a strong church.

Here are the eight ministries we developed:

Ministry in the Workplace
Ministry in the Home
Ministry in Church Life
Ministry in the Community
Ministry of Stewardship
Ministry of Mission and Witness
Ministry of Education
Ministry of Gifts and Leadership

Some weeks before, I had written to a few national leaders whom I knew to be interested in the issue of how local churches could be more empowering of laity. I had described our work in program and our desire now to address the question of structure. Bill Diehl, of the Riverbend Resource Center in Allentown, Pennsylvania, had responded with encouragement for our development of a clear mission statement. Mac Warford, President of Bangor Theological Seminary, had responded with eight pages on a theology of call and reflection on structure. So at this point in our process, we distributed copies of Warford's paper to the members of the task force and had them go off to read by themselves.

One of his comments in his reflections on structure provided the unifying vision we needed for our next step:

A point of recovery for the missionary character of the congregation is the rediscovery of the diaconate as the organizing center of the church's structure. In this sense, the diaconate becomes the unifying center which provides not simply for communion on Sunday, but integrates all the aspects of the church's life under the category of service.

Along with the richness of his reflection on call and structure, this comment enabled us to see a way to integrate, not just coordinate, the life of the church.

Our proposal is to create a single board called the Diaconate which will blend the policy and coordination functions of the present Church Council with the worship, sacrament, and spirituality functions of the present Diaconate. The new Diaconate will be composed of sixteen people plus a chairperson. Each of the eight ministries will be represented on the Diaconate by its chairperson and vice-chairperson.

The diagram on page 40 is an attempt to show concretely the vision of this new structure. Each ministry will have a four member committee plus the chairperson and vice chairperson, all elected by the congregation at its annual meeting. Each ministry might also have affiliated with it some task groups for specific functions, or volunteers carrying out aspects of its ministry. The design presumes that many decisions that are now made by committees will be delegated to individuals so that committees will spend less time on minutiae and more time in ministry development and planning.

Here are some examples of the kinds of responsibilities each ministry will have or might develop:

Ministry in the Workplace
Vocation and career
Ethics, justice
Retirement
Leadership
Youth vocational discernment

Ministry in the Home and Family
Parenting
Aging
Child care
Singles
Life cycle issues
Parenting one's parents

Ministry in Church Life
Community building
Hospitality
Cultivation of group life
Encouragement of members' participation in church life
(e.g., choirs, fellowship groups, social occasions)

Ministry in the Community
Service and advocacy on local issues
Public schools
Scouting, recreation, etc.

Proposed Structure for Mission

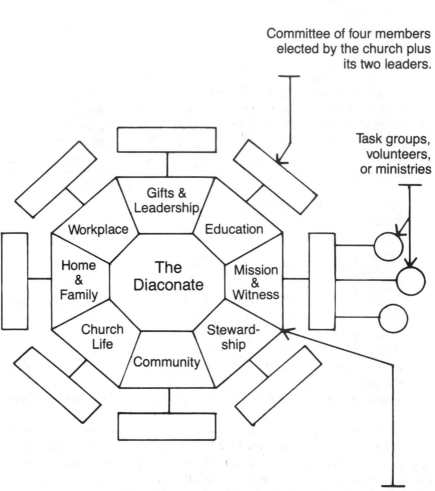

Committee of four members elected by the church plus its two leaders.

Task groups, volunteers, or ministries

Gifts & Leadership

Workplace

Education

Home & Family

The Diaconate

Mission & Witness

Church Life

Steward-ship

Community

The Diaconate, composed of two leaders from each ministry, elected by the church plus its chairperson who is also moderator of the church.

Housing issues
Caring ministries at times of need/crisis
Encouraging service on government/community boards

Ministry of Stewardship
Finance and budget matters
Property management
Investments
Pledge campaign

Ministry of Mission and Witness
Global mission promotion and interpretation
Citizenship issues (state and national)
Denominational relationships
Peace and justice
Advocacy

Ministry of Education
Sunday school
Intergenerational classes
Youth ministry
Confirmation program
Adult education
Consulting with other ministries on their educational programs

Ministry of Gifts and Leadership
Gifts identification
Leadership development
Helping committees be communities
Consulting with other ministries on their human resource needs

The task force had earlier made a list of every function in the life of the church. This list included everything from the smallest responsibility, like keeping closets clean, to the largest, like over-seeing investments. It included tangibles such as those two, but also intangibles like building parental support for youth programs and caring for persons' faith journeys. Now we began to assign those responsibilities to each of the ministry areas. This has served as a reality test for us: Just how much can a small group of people do? What can be delegated, what not? What needs to be done, what can be foregone?

The more the task force worked, the more opportunities they saw for the new design to build on its own strengths. For instance,

the ministry of gifts and leadership can be helpful to the community ministry in identifying persons to fill needs in town. The home
and family ministry can help educators understand the impact of
two-career families on children's spiritual development. The integration of all ministries through their presence in the Diaconate
will work to strengthen the church both as institution and as
empowering base for people's lives.

Further, the task force envisions asking every member or
family in the church to affiliate each September with one of the
ministries in workplace, home, church, or community. A husband
and wife might decide to affiliate this year with the workplace
ministry because they are approaching retirement and want to
learn and grow in preparation for that major change. Or in another
family, the husband might decide to affiliate with the home and
family ministry because he has been overworking and is feeling
the need for support for changing his lifestyle. His wife might
affiliate with the community ministry because she is already active
with the town's library board and wants to be better equipped to
give leadership there.

This process of annual affiliation will provide each ministry
with a known constituency for its programs and can enable the
church to be more responsive to the specific needs of its members.
The numbers of affiliated persons will also be helpful in our
deciding on staffing, program emphasis, and budget in any given
year as well.

There are probably a number of problems with our design.
The one we have identified most clearly is the size of the Diaconate. It is difficult to maintain attendance, energy, and common
vision in a body that large. It will also be a challenge to find
sixteen persons who are willing to give leadership to a ministry
and also serve on the Diaconate. However, we presently ask
chairpersons to serve on the Church Council as well as their own
committees, and this will be no more demanding than that. It may
well be that it will be easier to find leadership under the new
structure than the old since half of the ministries will be focused
on matters laity are already deeply concerned about.

I want to remind the reader that this structural design is brand
new and untested. It has only been through preliminary discussion.
It is by no means owned by the church, and may never be. It is
offered here only as an illustration of one church's struggle with
the issue of structural faithfulness, hopefully as a stimulus to other
churches to struggle with their own incarnation of the gospel in
their organizational structure.

CHAPTER V

The Renewal of the Church

I believe that mainline Protestantism is suffering from a revolution of declining expectations. Members attend church yearning for but not expecting a powerful experience of the worship of God and the integration of the faith with their daily lives. Churches receive new members yearning for but not expecting people who are alive to the faith and committed to living it out. Clergy are expected to live exemplary lives of faith, but there is a tacit agreement that it is unrealistic to expect laity to do the same.

This revolution of declining expectations is further exacerbated by the church's complicity. Membership in the Christian church has been watered down to a lowest common denominator of least offense. We dare not demand or expect anything from members or they will not join. In our fear-filled search for survival we guarantee our demise. In my experience, few people want to belong to something in which membership has no meaning. The higher we raise the expectations, the more likely it is that people of faith will gravitate toward us, not away. Colchester is in a good position to raise the standards of the meaning of membership. Demographically, we are going to grow. That means we can take the risk of increasing the expectations of members. The new members who affiliate during these years will have an entirely different understanding of the meaning and responsibility of church membership.

There will, of course, be some people who will not want to affiliate with a church that expects each of its members to minister. Yet membership in the Christian church must mean that, at least. Not everyone within our congregation is ready for every element of our program, and we have made it clear that they are welcome. However, the great weight of our emphasis will, we hope, gradually build a "critical mass" within the church. There has not been

opposition to the program, most likely because we have made
room for everyone to connect as they see fit. My hunch is that as
we near that critical mass, we may experience some conflict and
dissent. Both culture and structure of the church will gradually tilt
toward a standard of acceptable behavior and relation to the
church, and we will lose some people. Harsh as it may sound, I
would rather we lost people than we lose the faith. That is the
danger in the revolution of declining expectations.

Through the centuries, the sacraments have been prime loci
for renewal. They are ever the same, yet also radically open to
new understandings precisely because they bridge us into the
numinous realm of divine mystery.

As a congregation affiliated with the United Church of Christ
and the American Baptist Churches, we celebrate two sacraments,
baptism and communion. Both take on new meaning and new
power in relation to the ministry of the laity.

Baptism is the central rite of the church. It is the means of
admission and acceptance for all persons into the Body of Christ.
Unlike its predecessor rite, circumcision, it is not restricted to one
gender. It is available at all ages and under all conditions. In
baptism we receive the grace of God, are turned away from the
powers of death, and are all set apart for ministry.

The language of "set apart" has traditionally been used for
ordination. I believe that to be wrong. Every Christian has been set
apart for Christ and his ministry. The ordained minister is set in the
midst of those who have been set apart.

Work is a classically Calvinist theme, and altogether too pre-
dictable for a New England United Church of Christ ordained
minister to focus on. In the midst of all our emphasis on work, we
need the sacraments to remind us of God's grace. Robert Markus
draws on Augustinian thought to reflect on baptism as the rite that
"introduces the Christian into the new life of the age to come, and
hence also into the new order of work where the gulf between toil
and rest is closed."[16]

When we celebrate communion, we remember Jesus Christ, a
layperson who built a powerful lay movement that was threatening
to the religious authorities of his day and of every day since. He
offered us the sharing of bread and cup as an act of bonding
across time and space. With his words, "This is my body, broken
for you," he established us as the Body of Christ, willing also to be
broken for the sake of the world.

The "you" of whom he speaks is plural, not singular. The time
was coming in which his disciples would be scattered rather than

gathered, and communion ministers to the scattered Body as well
as to the gathered Body. Today we gather for worship and sacra
ment, then scatter for ministry, bonded by our shared communion.

Holy Communion is both deeply personal and profoundly
communal, thus moving us beyond the individualism which so
plagues American Christians. Unfortunately even this most sacred
of ordinances has become contaminated and is often received in
keeping with a privatistic culture. We hear the words "broken for
you" as spoken to the individual. We receive the sacrament in a
privatized world of relation between "me and my God." As the
corporate nature of faith is understood more deeply by covenant
groups and church leaders working with the management system,
communion is a sustaining force, and takes on new meaning. As
communicants gain a sense that they are sent out to carry the
gospel into the public arena of life as well as the private, the social
power of the sacrament is restored.

Holy communion is a moment to reflect on the way in which
God ministers to us and grants us grace. For when our days are
filled with work, then worship (and particularly the mystical oneness with Christ and one another which is ours in communion) can
restore our sense of balance, renew our baptism and close the gulf
between toil and rest.

The church's renewal also requires the liberation of the laity
from the church systems which keep them marginalized. None of
us would claim that the people of Colchester are oppressed in the
same sense in which the poor of the third world are. They live in
hunger and poverty. Exploitation and oppression are not rhetoric
for them, but harsh realities of life. The middle-class comfort of
Colchester stands in marked contrast to the daily life of a Latin
American member of comunidad de base, or Christian base community. Yet the liberation theology which has grown out of their
experience and their perspective on the faith offers a way of
viewing our work in restoring ministry to the laity.

Within the Church, the laity have become marginalized and
are in need of liberation from the systems which keep them there.
The Christian faith and the practice of ministry have come to be
the province of the clergy. That is an untenable position, inherently
contradicting central teachings of the faith itself. The approach
described here is informed by, infused with and indebted to the
spirit of liberation theology and liberation practice.

In liberation theology, the development of a liberating practice is central: a living out in action of the faith which has come
down to us in the tradition. Liberation theology takes the world,

not the church, as the locus of God's action. It hears the words of John 3:16 and takes them as powerful truth: "For God so loved the world…" that God sent Jesus Christ to be God-incarnate in the midst of political, economic, and spiritual oppression. It is this world-facing spirituality of liberation theology that is at one and the same time most misunderstood and most needed by the contemporary church. It is this world-facing spirituality that informs our work in the ministry of the laity.

There are four key ways this project aligns with liberation theology. First, we begin with people where they are most invested. Just as Paolo Freire taught peasants in the north of Brazil to read by working with them on the digging of a well, which meant new life to them, so we begin by taking seriously the workdays of our members.[17] That is where they have invested themselves most in time and energy. By beginning there, in the midst of their lives, we take them seriously as full persons. Instead of beginning with a Bible study, in which laity invariably feel ill at ease and without authority, we begin with them sharing with one another about their work, a matter in which they have considerable authority. Later, we begin to develop the Biblical connection which helps them see that the issues that are real for them in their work lives are spoken to in the book of the faith.

Our experience has been that this process of moving from life to text (instead of text to life) frees people to a new vantage point on both life and faith. Suddenly they see how the faith sheds light on every aspect of life, and they become evangelical in their excitement about the gospel. They experience a conversion and become themselves evangelists for the ministry of all God's people.

The second key element we share with liberation theology is a willingness to utilize the tools the world has to offer. Theology is done hand in hand with cultural critique. Consideration of the theme of principalities and powers uses both the Biblical text and power analysis. Because laity are better versed in the languages of their workplaces, we tend to back into the use of scriptural language. It comes alive for them when we use the skills they have from their own work to analyze a situation, and only then gives it its Christian name or compares it with the way Jesus or a prophet analyzed a particular condition. The tools that have been developed in business and industry, in public schools, and Y.W.C.A.'s are the products of human minds, minds blessed with gifts from God. So we receive them as ministries from those institutions to us. All God's people minister, and their bases of ministry are only rarely the local church.

The third key element shared with liberation theology is a focus on action. Reflection is an important ingredient, but it is not the ultimate end of an undertaking. Action in the world is central. Since a major element of our program focuses on work, and presumes the workplace as a potential locus for ministry, action is presupposed. The participants live out the faith through their daily lives and come together in a support community twice a month to analyze and critique their ministries, to support one another, to worship and celebrate. This rhythm of action—reflection—action is critically important to the success of the program. It grounds the faith dimension in the truth of human life as it is in fact lived. Further, it has been as the first Covenant Group has gone out to other churches and places to promote the ministry of the laity that they have made it fully their own. The challenge of action and articulation has deepened their reflection.

The final element of liberation theology which we share is the seriousness with which structures and systems are taken. Rather than seeing this as an attitude adjustment problem, we see the ministry of the laity as a systemic and structural issue for the whole church. The marginalization of the laity is not solely in the attitude of the clergy. It is also in the way the local church is structured to pull people in and to build itself up as an institution. As long as these are 'come' (rather than 'go') structures that we support, so long will the clergy be dominant and the laity marginal. As long as we define the church as the body that gathers for worship on Sunday morning and not the body that scatters for ministry through the week, so long will the clergy be dominant. As long as the local church structures itself for administration of the institution and not for mission as the Body of Christ, so long will the clergy be dominant—even if they do not feel that they are, or want to be.

Just as the *comunidades de base* in Latin America must spend time in analysis of economic conditions as they study the Bible, so must support communities in the ministry of the laity spend time in analysis of the structural reasons for their marginalization as they grow in faith. Action to change those structural realities must occur, or else the marginalization is exacerbated by programs on the fringe of the ongoing life of the institution. That is the reason for the introduction of the management system and our proposal for a new structure for our congregation. These have grown out of discussions in the Covenant Groups and in the Diaconate. Now as they are implemented further, there will be continuing opportunities for laity to share with one another their different analyses and strategies. The action that we take together will prompt reflection and more action. Eventually the management system and the structure will bear little resemblance to that described here. Change in design is inevitable, and desirable when it signals ownership.

The renewal of the church is a perennial subject. Many prescriptions have been written over the centuries. Most have focused on the role of the laity in the faith. During the 1950s and 1960s the World Council of Churches gave sustained attention to the ministry of the laity, and I commend their work to the reader. The theological work of Hendrik Kraemer and the work on structures reported in The Church for Others and the Church for the World are particularly helpful.[18] Colchester's work is one attempt to bring the best of decades of thought about renewal to bear on the life of one congregation.

CHAPTER VI

On Work

Barbara Wheeler argues in her article "What kind of Leadership for Tomorrow's Churches?"

> that the wrenching changes mainline Protestantism is now expe-
> riencing raise radical questions about what their products should
> be. Will the same religious goods and services that met the needs
> of the mostly white, middle-to-upper-middle class, family-
> oriented churches through most of their American history meet
> today's demands for inclusiveness, for ethnic pluralism, for
> attention to changing social roles and structures?[19]

The response we give to that question is "No". Our churches
are built on the assumption of a society that has not existed for
several decades, a society of small cooperative communities in
which work, family, and leisure were integrated. In that setting, the
local parish intersected with life at its most significant points.
Today, we live in a fragmented society. Major portions of church
members' lives are spent on the road and at work. Neighborhood
and family are places of refuge from the stress of "real" life. The
exclusive association of the church with places of refuge renders
the church powerless to confront life at its most significant points
for most people. Neighborhood and town were once the locale of
work and public life, but are no longer. Now work and public life
are lived on a larger stage. And the church is left in the wings.

For several decades the churches continued to address some
of the real issues of life for families. During those years women continued to stay at home. For them, work, family, and leisure continued
to focus in neighborhood or town.[20] Women, we notice, continued to
connect to the church. Men did not. Their issues were no longer
addressed.

With the widening participation of women in the workforce, however, the "religious goods and services" which traditional parishes have to offer are increasingly irrelevant to both genders.

The significant points of life are found in relation to work. There, issues of identity, vocation, and meaning interact with one's place in a hierarchy of value concretely measured every payday. There the public issues of corporate responsibility and justice, of peacemaking and economic conversion, of pluralism and economic power are lived out in each person's daily life, albeit on dramatically different scales from job to job.

Our ministry represents an attempt to discover the ways a local church can organize itself to intersect with the work world and reconnect again with the issues with which our members are struggling. Over these years, we have attempted to introduce the public dimensions of the faith. As the church addresses work issues, it is dealing with issues which are significant for everyone, even those who are retired and often ready to reflect on the meaning of all those years of work. Work, insofar as it carries people beyond the places of refuge and into participation in the economic commonwealth, is a public dimension of our lives. It pulls people into the marketplace.

It is my observation, however, that work is increasingly experienced by workers as a private activity. In the commuter and computer age, large numbers of the workforce leave their private homes, drive their private cars, and arrive at their private offices or work stations. They have little sense of participation there in the public world, or of the broader implications and consequences of their particular jobs. This makes the work of the local church all the more critical. "Equipping the saints for the work of ministry" must include the ability to critique and overcome the privatization of American society. As workers allow themselves to divorce even their work from connection to the larger arenas of public responsibility, they participate in the dehumanization of the workplace, the disempowerment of workers and the loss of a public ethic.[21]

One of my reservations about our program is its emphasis on individual experience in the workplace and individual experience of the faith. An early decision to introduce the public dimension of faith in a way which connected personally to their lives (specifically through attention to work) has contributed to this problem. By focusing on the individual's experience we risk validating the culture of individualism, which runs counter to the Judaeo-Christian tradition. Theologically, if we understand the Church as the Body of Christ, we must be developing ways to be a Body, a community, not just an aggregate collection of individuals.

Although group experience is central to the program, and although covenant is a central concept, still individual behavior is the focus. At times the covenant groups have been able to break through to communal life (e.g., their decision to give themselves as a group to a year of promoting the ministry of the laity beyond our congregation). More attention needs to be paid to the bonds that the groups build in the first several months. "Personal" and "communal" do not stand in tension with one another. The objective is to make the program deeply personal yet not individualistic.

The privatization of American life and faith has yielded an alienation from public issues. Even when dealing with work, the introduction of justice issues or global implications at times seems forced, despite the fact that all workplaces are filled with opportunities for seeing the connections between one's personal situation and the situations of others, near or far. The public issues, the larger arena, seem to have nothing to do with a person's sense of self. Here is a great challenge for our program: to overcome the privatization in such a way that the public becomes a matter of personal life and faith.

In Colchester the distance between person and public issue in the workplace comes in part because most of our members are middle level people. They have not experienced the most dehumanizing of workplace injustices, such as a textile or mine worker might. They also have little power to change the larger systemic contributions to the injustice that affects everyone. Caught in the middle, they simply do their jobs as best they can, as fairly as they can, causing the least harm possible. ("I try and do as well as I can, without hurting anybody," is the way one member put it.)

Clearly participants in our program gain a new perspective on the faith, and new energy for ministry. They begin to see that faith is related to all dimensions of their lives. We need to help them better understand how their lives and their faith are a part of the larger whole, directly related to social issues, and to political and economic conditions in a global perspective.

The management system can challenge us to address these larger issues by its attention to systems. As people are trained to think systemically in the church, they can be led to apply that thinking to their work lives and to the larger society. One of the virtues of working on both program and system at the same time is that they can strengthen and reinforce each other in thought patterns, collective lifestyle, and value-based decision-making.

There is, however, a dilemma in focusing on work. While it does enable us to connect with the daily lives of most people, such a focus leaves out those who are outside the traditional workforce, and even some within it.

Speaking of the workplace as setting for ministry is easy when addressing the work of teachers, health care workers, and those who work in offices. For those who are production workers, however, the connections are more difficult to make. The pursuit of excellence in one's work is certainly one avenue, and the issue of the worthiness of the product is another. Yet most production workers are precisely those who are most caught and least able to change jobs. When we address the worthiness of the product in Christian value terms, sometimes we simply add to the burdens of an already frustrated believer.

Most production workers do have some opportunities for interaction on the job. They face issues every day of whether to set aside their own production quota to help someone else, or whether to buck management on the way they have established the work this time. They are often unionized and must weigh the level of their participation in the union. There are myriad opportunities for ministry for production workers. However, they must be identified concretely and frequently in order for any of us to see them.

Although we have proportionally fewer blue collar workers in our congregation now as a result of the direction of population growth in the town, we still consider their presence important to the way we carry out our ministry of the laity program. Finding programmatic approaches that value them and are relatively comfortable for them is a justice issue within the church. If anyone will become invisible in mainline Protestantism in the next decade, it will be the production worker. Programs in the ministry of the laity can be helpful to them and to the church if undertaken with sensitivity to their issues and their needs. They can be alienating if not. The management system helps us overcome that process of alienation by orienting us to the task of enabling the ministries of all God's people through the whole work of the church. Thus, awareness of this issue can be worked through the system to result in changes in the way we do leadership development, the varieties of educational approaches we use, the way we run our meetings.

Another constituency that can have difficulty with our emphasis on the workplace is homemakers. Even though we have tried to emphasize that workplace does not mean only places of paid work, still the message is mixed. There are few written or video resources on homemaking as ministry. Only three participants out of twenty in the Covenant Groups have been homemakers. We do not have much new light to shed.

However, one of our Covenant Group members, after much struggling with her own adjustment to fulltime homemaking after some years in a professional career, and after much thinking about mothering as ministry, has begun a special ministry with mothers in our community. Two support and learning groups have been formed, one daytime and one evening. We expect that new insights will be forthcoming and will affect the way we design and promote future program.

Finally, it is important to note that a focus on work in relation to ministry can complicate pastoral relationships.

In positive terms, it opens doors to new understandings of the lives of members. Pastoral visitation at places of work or at lunch breaks is a gift of caring totally unlike a visit at home. Deepening one's understanding of work issues in a person's life diversifies the illustrations available for preaching, and the occasions available for pastoral care and teaching.

However, few people are truly happy in their work, and trying to get them to see their work as ministry may simply set them up for more frustration. Sometimes a person who has been unhappy at work can, through the ministry of the laity program, see a new dimension of meaning and new opportunities for self-giving there. Very often, however, focusing on work shines a spotlight on an aspect of life a person would just as soon ignore. The process we use for identifying gifts in combination with my administration of the Myers-Briggs Type Indicator has been helpful as people have begun to think through the conflicts between their gifts and their work. A pastor needs to be prepared to learn as much as possible as fast as possible about the fields of career and vocation guidance, and the many resources now available. If a pastor is fortunate, he or she will have in the congregation a member or two who have experience in personnel, guidance counseling, or out-placement. Barring that good fortune, these are areas in which training must be sought, either for oneself, or for a parishioner.

The nature and locus of work have changed dramatically in our society in recent decades. The church has failed to keep step and is suffering a consequent irrelevance to its members' lives. A focus on ministry in the workplace offers both opportunity and dilemma in rectifying that circumstance. Despite some negative effects, our experience in Colchester would seem to validate the claim that pastors and churches must pay significantly more attention to the workday lives of the scattered church.

CHAPTER VII

Management, Systems, and Ministry

It has come to be popular to describe the role of ordained ministers in the renewed church as "equippers of the saints." I have come to question this model insofar as it implies that equipping is a one-way street. In fact, the laity in Colchester have done as much to equip me as I have to equip them. They have taught me about their lives and about the shape of work as we move into the last decade of the twentieth century. They have taught me skills in education, group process, organizational development, and leadership training. Sometimes this has been intentional teaching on their part. Often it has been their willingness to express a need, and their desire for me to respond to that need. We have equipped one another for ministry.

When I began to think about the management system component of this project, I was motivated by a concern about what would happen to the vision of a renewed church that empowers the ministry of the laity if I were to leave. I knew that the core of leaders in the church owned the vision, so this was not a case of my imposing my legacy on my successor. It was a question of how to incarnate the vision so that the laity would be structurally empowered to carry it on. As we have seen, change which is not institutionalized is lost in a short time.

To my surprise, the more I worked on the management system, the more committed I became to staying in Colchester. I was putting something in place so that I could leave, and now I did not need to leave. I no longer felt that my work here was done. If anything, my sense of calling to this specific time and place deepened. What happened?

Many laity from other congregations have told me and members of our Covenant Groups that they believe their pastor would "never stand for" this kind of program and system. I have indeed encountered some clergy who are threatened by our work. However, I suspect that laity are often just as threatened, and use the pastor as the excuse.

My own experience has been to find myself liberated of a great many burdens. I am no longer the one person expected to do theological reflection. Now within our congregation, there is a whole community of people who understand something about how difficult it is to do ministry. An entire new field of inquiry and pastoral relationship has opened up before me. I have no lack of new sermon illustrations, and always know that a good proportion of the congregation is actually listening to what I have to say from the pulpit. I am challenged in my personal and professional growth to learn new leadership and interaction skills and styles. Several times a year I get to listen to laity preach about the relation between their faith and their daily lives, and receive new theological and biblical insights from them. Twenty or thirty people are fired up about the faith and the church in a way I could never have dreamed. What more could any pastor want, except perhaps a whole church like this?

The prospect of spending the next several years working on the conversion of the church, not just individuals, is exciting. I believe this is one of the most profound implications of this project for the ordained ministry. It is not only that it renews one's relationship with the individuals in one's congregation, but also that it leads one into new clarity about the pastor as leader of a system that can be changed. The ordained minister is an organizational leader as well as a pastor to individuals. As such, we are called to cure the soul of the church as well as individual persons, to convert the institution as well as individuals. In the midst of the day-to-day crises of parish ministry, it is easy to lose sight of that calling.

It is not always easy to serve as organizational leader in the midst of a people who are empowering one another to ministry. There are many fine lines to be walked. It would be easy to step back and bow out, saying, "It's up to them now. All I need to do is serve." To do so is to abdicate leadership, to fail to minister in the midst of the very people who have called one to do just that. Instead of what is often called enabling ministry (and can sometimes degenerate into the foregoing abdication), I wish to affirm a style that emphasizes empowerment and vision. Management does not consist only in problem-solving and implementing, but also in pathfinding (see page 9).

The ordained minister is set in the midst of a people to empower them to build themselves up as a self-consciously Chris-

tian community set free to ministries of reconciliation and transformation in the world. Rather than equipping individual saints, in
this model the pastor's role is to build a theologically informed
community that develops, together, a reflective practice of ministry.
The visionary empowering leader offers a coherent vision of the
church and the world as they were meant to be, invites people to
share that vision and to use their gifts in enabling it to become
reality. Together we develop a collective analysis of what is keeping us from the vision and a strategy for getting there. Together we
discover the gifts we each have to offer, and encourage each other
in the use of those gifts in both world and church.

This is not a style of leadership that will work for one who is
timid. Nor will it work for one who must be in control. However, I
believe the Holy Spirit is calling every ordained minister beyond
timidity and beyond control into a new life lived in rich relationship with those who are called the laity.

The visionary empowering leader must have the courage to
offer a vision and the confidence to build a process of inclusion
that results in both change in the vision and its consequent ownership by the church. Nothing less will suffice.

In some cases, a visionary empowering leader will have to
learn to be directive for a while, to tolerate dependency for the
time being, to create the space and time in which a new vision can
take root. We live in the "time between the times" when the dominion of God is only breaking in and not fully present. Impa-
tience will only strengthen the grip of the old ways, not loosen it.
The vision aspect of our leadership keeps us on a cutting edge.
The empowerment mandate keeps us in touch with the people
and where they are. Both must be true of us or we cannot lead.

From time to time in the course of this project, I have had a
glimmer of insight into the way the church acts as a training
ground for its members. Through planning and attention to systems, we have given a core of our members a sense of what it
means to participate in changing an organization for the good. The
skills they develop in relation to the church carry over into other
arenas. It goes beyond that as well.

It seems to me that the most explicitly public dimension of the
church is its organizational life. Rather than the stands it takes on social
issues or the degree to which it allows public use of its facilities, it is
its way of organizing itself that speaks of its attitude toward the world
and determines whether it will be missional or static. It is through
participation in organizational life that members are drawn out of
their private worlds into consideration of the larger good.

Therefore addressing the way the local church is organized is a publicly responsible act. If the church's structures and systems do not reflect its mission, then they must be changed. Form must follow function.

We have to recognize that the churches have developed into "waiting churches" into which people are expected to come. Its inherited structures stress and embody this static outlook. One may say that we are in danger of perpetuating 'come structures' instead of replacing them by 'go structures.'[22]

The "morphological fundamentalism" which J. C. Hoekendijk and Hans Schmidt first described in 1962 still reigns supreme. They refer to a "rigid and inflexible attitude toward the morphe (structure, "Gestalt") of the congregation similar to the attitude prevailing in biblical fundamentalism."[23] Though many of our churches have tinkered with internal design, and have indeed made progress in organizational development terms, few have even considered the larger questions of 'come' and 'go' structures.

Colchester is still a 'come' structure. We have begun to ask some of the significant questions. We have begun to conduct some of the right programs. We have put a temporary body in place to begin work on some of the issues. But for now Colchester is still a 'come' structure.

To become a 'go' structure, a true church of Jesus Christ, we must think in new ways and take new risks. That is the purpose of the management system. It forces us to identify issues we would otherwise ignore. It causes different portions of the system to challenge one another. It takes a coherent vision of the church and incarnates it in a comprehensive system so that no part of the church's life is untouched. Precisely because it is comprehensive and pervasive, it will take years to accomplish.

The organization of the church's life is a major contributor to the way its members apprehend the faith. If we speak one way, but live corporately another, it is the lived message that is most strongly received. Our present work has tried to build a foundation on which a new corporate and public life might be built.

Each year we have ended our Covenant Group with time for each member to reflect individually on where she or he was going from that point on, both in relation to ministry/work and in relation to the church. We have also pressed the question of where the group as a whole has wanted to go, and where they felt the church ought to go.

As we have reflected on our progress in supporting the ministry of the laity, we have begun to believe that the discipline of asking this question is crucial. Both program and management system are future oriented. Every component is seen as foundational for next steps. This has enabled both individuals and church to keep growing.

The cutting edges for Colchester Federated Church in the next several years will be the full implementation of the management system and new structure, the development of the vocation and career center, creative use of the occasion of membership growth, and an expansion of the church's understanding of its mission in the community and region. The first three are clearly described here. The last needs explication.

Thus far, our work on the ministry of the laity has not pulled people very far out of their comfortable worlds. It has deepened their faith and developed their leadership, but it has done that within their normal day-to-day lives. Yet Christian ministry draws us outside ourselves, demands of us self-criticism and cultural critique. If our ministry will address the needs of "the least of these" and will speak of God's love for the world, then we must be continually having new experiences of that world. If we are going to build a true church in the image of Jesus Christ, we need to find ways to challenge people on their assumptions about where ministry can take them.

Two approaches are needed. One is already being designed into future Covenant Group programs, and that is the urban immersion experience. The second must be a very concrete mission engagement which brings members of the church into encounter with a world that is beyond theirs: developing or rehabilitating low-income housing; a hospice for AIDS patients; action against racism; partnership in mission with an organization in Uganda; any of these would work.

Every church needs a rhythm of movement between corporate ministry and individual ministry, between nurturing members within their own spheres of need and drawing them out beyond themselves, between institutional renewal for the sake of the world and institutional abandonment for the sake of the world. This mission component is a crucial next step.

CONCLUSION

One of the questions the Diaconate began to ask during their study of the management system was "How do we connect the ministry of the laity with our structure and with everything we do in the church and outside the church?" That is the question which we have attempted to answer in our design and implementation of a management system supporting the ministry of the laity. Program, process, and organizational structure have been evaluated and means devised for integrating them into a systemic approach to management of this local church.

This report is of necessity incomplete. It will be several years before the full results are known and in place. Yet there is high ownership of the problems and the opportunities by our church's leadership, and specific responsibilities have been accepted. We believe we are working on some of the most important issues facing Christianity today. The faithfulness with which we are able to pursue the implications of our insights will affect not only our local church, but others as well.

Yet it is imperative that the reader understand that this work is deeply rooted in Colchester. The program and management system are not and cannot be a blueprint for the church in any other context. Our particular set of problems and opportunities are not another's. The implications for another church can only be perceived in attention to the details of persons' lives, to the socio-economic context, and to the development of a strategy faithful to the gospel, to persons, and to the cultural milieu in which the church finds itself.

Finally, I must confess to a certain nervousness that those who read this book will decide to visit Colchester, expecting to find here a church that has all the answers. We do not. Even while we have begun to discover some of the right questions, we are still moving haltingly toward the vision of an Empowering Church. For many years we will be living into our hope, faltering here and there along the way like any human institution. We take hope from the Spirit and from our life together in a loving community of faith.

Questions for Committees

The following questions were developed to encourage existing boards and committees in the life of the church to see the intersection between their work and the ministry of the laity. They were also useful in disciplining ourselves to discern whether the present structures of the church could serve adequately to empower the ministry of the laity.

Diaconate

Charged with the spiritual well-being of the church, the Diaconate might be charged to look at issues like:

1. The worship life of the church: What are the points at which we could make the ministry of the laity come to life? Should laity participate weekly in worship, or will that (as Anderson and Jones contend) draw them away from a sense of their own ministries? Might there be special occasions that could be created to celebrate different vocations and ministries? Should we be considering a local ordination/validation service for those who wish it? Could we restructure the entire worship service in some way that would really give members a sense of being sent forth?

2. The sacraments: What would happen if we gave the diaconate members a more prominent role in baptism and communion? What might it be? Should we require more than the present one-session meeting with the ordained minister before a baptism? We also now ask parents of infants/children being baptized to come to church several times before we set a baptism date. Should this be continued? What kind of follow-up should be made with families after a baptism? By whom? When?

3. Confirmation: Is there any way to establish a relation with young people during confirmation/initiation to adulthood so that they see the church as a resource for life decisions? How can we help confirmands begin their life in the church with an understanding of ministry?

4. Young adult ministry: Might we not offer the church as a resource for life/work planning? How could that be done? Is this not a prime time for the riches of the church to be brought to bear? What if we were able to find ways for members established in

professions/work areas to mentor younger members, or for younger members to shadow older as they consider possible life works?

5. Pastoral care and parish care: How might members of the church be encouraged to know each other's work lives better? Can people be brought together in work-similar groups for support? How can the clergy know more about members' work lives? How might the church's concern for vocational well-being be extended beyond our own church?

6. Membership: We already spend some time having new members identify their gifts for us. What if we had them identify their gifts for each other? How about changing our whole approach to membership classes and spending major time on gifts identification, ministry discernment, learning about each other's work lives, families, faith?

Business Committee

Charged with responsibility for finance and properties, the Business Committee might look at some of the following:

1. Financial management: What does the stewardship of the church's money have to do with the way we earn our livings? With the way others earn theirs? Should we be looking at where our money is invested in relation to how those corporations do or do not live out the values we believe in?

2. Budget: What does our budget say about our values? About our priorities? Should there be a line item specifically for the ministry of the laity? Is there a way to do budget building and financial management without so much expenditure of time and energy? Or would that turn it into a routine operation and devalue it as a theological enterprise?

3. Properties: Is there a way any of our buildings might be used to develop the ministry of the laity? To give support to those who are hurting?

Human Resources

Charged with responsibility for identification of gifts, nomination of

leaders, and leadership development, the Human Resources Committee is already looking at some of the following:

1. Gifts identification: Besides simply accepting what people
have to say about their gifts, is there a way to deepen their awareness of their own specific gifts? Besides using those gifts in service
to the church, is there a way to encourage them in consciousness
of the use of their gifts in the rest of their lives?

2. Nominations: We already have job descriptions for every
volunteer job in the church. Maybe we should develop job descriptions for every member in relation to their lives "outside" the
church. When a person is nominated/elected, how could they be
helped to see their position as a ministry? How can leaders be
helped to know the gifts of members of their committees?

3. Leadership development: We already provide a two hour
workshop of leadership training on the Sunday of installation for
all committee members, and a similar length workshop for chairpersons. What ongoing development do leaders need? And how
might we enhance the transferability of that learning to their work
and community and family lives?

Stewardship and Mission

Charged with responsibility for encouraging members in the
stewardship of their financial resources and for promoting the
mission of the church beyond Colchester, this committee should
look at:

1. Stewardship: How does the way people earn their dollars
relate to how they spend/give them? Does the stewardship of the
rest of a person's resources (talents, life, etc.) relate to this committee's self-understanding? If people had a sense of the stewardship of their total lives, would that change the way they dealt with
their money and related to the church? Are there some ways of
raising the lifestyle questions in relation to ministry of the laity in
the home?

2. Mission: When people say they don't care, or don't feel
connected to the world beyond their neighborhood, what does this
imply about their sense of self? Of community? Of faith? Of power?
Is there any sense in which Colchester Federated Church has a

mission at Pratt and Whitney? at Aetna? at Backus Hospital? If we were to engage people in a new way of looking at the mission of the church and connect that to their workplaces would that help them feel empowered? What if we were to start the other way around, and help people get in touch with their feelings about their work, their workplace, their coworkers, their corporations? Then help them make connections to people in developing nations? in southern milltowns? in cities like Hartford?

Outreach

Charged with responsibility for the ministry of this church to its community, and for encouraging members in their ministry as citizens, Outreach might look at:

1. Ministry to the community: Who are the people in our church who have chosen ministry through voluntarism and public service in our community? How might others be encouraged? Could a link be made to Human Resources in relation to gifts identification, and to Diaconate for commissioning? Are there some who would like to serve but need help in organizing a ministry to convalescent homes, group homes, the homeless, the poor, battered women, whoever? We already have identified child care, housing, and poverty as major issues for our town. How might people be brought to see these as personal ministry opportunities? as corporate ministry opportunities? Does this church have a mission at local industries, businesses, restaurants? Who carries on that ministry? Do they know it?

2. Citizen ministry: What is the role of the church in mobilizing its members when there is a local, state, or national issue that needs their attention? What are the limits? How might we help people to see citizen advocacy as a ministry? Who are the people who are already doing this now? How might they be supported and strengthened in their work?

Board of Religious Education

Charged with responsibility for children, youth, and adult education, this board can look at:

1. Children: How can we raise our children with different assumptions about the church and the ministry? When they are

with us in worship? When they worship separately? When they are in class? Can we give them a sense of ministry through school? What would happen if the laity who lead them in worship on occasion were introduced to the children in terms of their work/ministries and spoke to the children about what that means to them?

2. Youth: Through church school, confirmation, and youth groups, we have many opportunities to reach youth. Do we reach them with this message? Can they be empowered to understand their school lives, after-school work lives, family lives as ministry opportunities? Can they be challenged around life/work issues? Can we give them a safe space to explore work options before they commit themselves to degree programs or apprenticeships? What might their ministries to the church be? to adults in the church?

3. Adults: As we educate adults in Bible study, faith, personal growth and witness, social issues, what are the opportunities to help them connect to ministry? Is there a difference between educating for discipleship and educating for ministry? Are there skills and content that people have learned in their worklives that they might be willing to teach others through the church? As a person comes to a new awareness of ministry and its challenges in his/her life, what kind of support is needed? Can we use the Myers-Briggs fruitfully with adults as with young adults? For addressing job change, family and interpersonal, mid-life crisis, retirement issues?

Excerpt from Some Notes on Planned Social Change
by Jackson W. Carroll, Hartford Seminary

4. Factors Facilitating Acceptance of Planned Change

From the experience of various persons involved in planned change as participants, consultants, researchers, etc., there has developed a number of generalizations or hypotheses regarding acceptance or rejection of change. Some of these are quite obvious and common-sensical. Some (perhaps most) hold only under certain conditions—"other things being equal". In this final section, it will perhaps be useful to provide an outline summary of a number of these generalizations that seem to be especially appropriate for planned change in church systems. I have drawn the propositions from a variety of sources in addition to personal experience. I have not, however, attempted to cite the sources, since they generally are shared and expressed in a variety of sources. (It should be noted that an especially helpful summary on which I have drawn in part is provided by Goodwin Watson, "Resistance to Change", pp. 117-131 in Gerald Zaltman, et.al., eds., *Processes and Phenomena of Social Change,* New York: John Wiley and Sons, 1973). I present the generalizations without elaborating on or illustrating them.

4.1 Characteristics of the Proposed Change

(1) Changes are more likely to be accepted when they are perceived to be based on values, norms, theories, and concepts compatible with those of the organization or persons involved.

(2) Innovations that are functionally incompatible with existing organizational arrangements will have low probability of implementation unless the organizational arrangements are altered to accomodate the innovation.

(3) The less the proposed change is perceived to threaten the security and autonomy of the participants, the greater the likelihood of acceptance.

(4) Those benefits that the proposed change offers that other alternatives do not offer are its "critical attributes." The larger the number of critical attributes and the greater their magnitude, the more likely the change is to be accepted.

(5) A change is more likely to be widely accepted if it is seen as reducing rather than adding to the burdens of the participants.

(6) A change that offers new and interesting experience for participants will have a greater probability of acceptance.

(7) The greater the pervasiveness of the change (i.e., requiring broad changes and adjustments in various elements of the organization) the slower its acceptance will be.

(8) Changes that can be introduced incrementally or piecemeal are more easily accepted than those requiring sudden, large scale alterations.

(9) The simpler and easier an innovation is to understand and put into operation (especially the latter), the more likely it will be accepted. However, regardless of simplicity and ease of operation, the change will not succeed if members do not understand it or lack the skills and resources to use it.

(10) Change will be more readily accepted when there are visible examples of other similar systems (preferably nearby) that have successfully adopted the change.

(11) A change that can be tried on a limited basis without entirely abandoning current practice has a higher probability of acceptance than one that is irreversible; however, innovations that can be tried on a limited basis have a greater likelihood of being abandoned in favor of the status quo ante.

(12) The more the change strategy is perceived to be open and amenable to revision if experience indicates need for revision, the more likely it is to be accepted.

4.2 Who Brings the Change and How it is Brought

(1) The greater the sense of ownership of the change strategy and process by persons involved in the system, and the less it appears that the strategy is devised and operated by outsiders, the more likely the change will be accepted.

(2) Change is more likely to be accepted if those undergoing the change feel that their knowledge, traditions, and skills are treated as valuable and important; however, they will resist change when they are made to feel that they are recipients of superior knowledge and skill coming from outside their situation.

(3) A change strategy that has the wholehearted endorsement and support of top leaders of the system (e.g., pastor and lay leaders) has a considerably higher probability of success than one lacking their full support.

(4) While change will be more readily accepted in an organization when it has the support of "gatekeepers" (the power structure), "gatekeepers" are nevertheless likely to resist changes that call for pervasive restructuring of the organization.

4.3 Procedures in Initiating and Implementing Change

(1) In general, consensual or participative styles of decision-making facilitate acceptance of change more readily than authoritative or top down decision-making.

(2) While consensual or participative decision-making may be important for gaining acceptance and support for a change, it will be dysfunctional unless authority and accountability for initiating and implementing innovations are clearly defined.

(3) Decisions to adopt change strategies made by top leaders (authority decisions) are usually more efficient in getting the innovation off the ground; however, changes initiated by the authoritative approach are more likely to be discontinued than those brought about by a consensual or participative approach.

(4) Authoritative (top down) decisions to change will be effective only when one and preferably several of the following factors are present: (a) the "authority" has resources that the persons affected by the change do not have; (b) there is a crisis situation requiring immediate action; (c) there is little hostility to or mistrust of the "authority"; (d) the change is not complex or extensive; (e) persons are already motivated to accept the change (or motivation is not important); (f) there is clearly no reasonable possibility for a consensual or participative solution.

(5) A change will more likely be accepted when participants have joined in diagnostic efforts and had opportunity to reach a consensus on the basic problem(s) and its importance.

(6) The more fully proponents of the change empathize with and recognize the valid objections of opponents of the change, the more possible it is to take steps to reduce unnecessary fears and enhance acceptance.

(7) The likelihood of acceptance of change will be increased when changes are based on clear goals and objectives, clear guidelines for implementing the changes, and have built in evaluative and feedback methods.

(8) Acceptance and institutionalization of change will be facilitated if there is at least one early and visible success in the

implementation process. The magnitude of the success relative to the goals for the change is not as important as the timing and visibility of the success.

(9) If regular opportunities for feedback of participants' perceptions of the proposed and actual change are provided, there will be less likelihood that misinformation and misunderstanding will subvert implementation of the change.

(10) Change will more likely persist (be institutionalized) where organizational positions (roles) are established that are accountable for implementing the change and where necessary resources for its implementation are allocated on a continuing basis.

4.4 Summary Proposition Regarding Readiness for Change

The more a change appears to participants to be a major intervention into the status quo, the more it threatens to overthrow existing values and norms, the more it appears to be in conflict with what is comfortable or safe, the greater the resistance that will have to be overcome. However, there will be a readiness to accept or implement change where the participants see the change to be in their own best interests, where the change is consistent with their values and norms, and where the capacity to act is present or developable without high dependency on someone else or some other system.

1. William E. Diehl, *Thank God It's Monday* (Philadelphia: Fortress Press, 1982).

2. Ibid.

3. For a helpful treatment of the interaction of identity, context, program, and process in a church's life, see Jackson W. Carroll, Carl S. Dudley, and William McKinney, *Handbook for Congregational Studies* (Nashville: Abingdon, 1986).

4. Harold J. Leavitt, "Management and Management Education," The Stockton Lecture, London Business School, March 16, 1983, cited in Joseph C. Hough, Jr. and John B. Cobb, Jr., *Christian Identity and Theological Education* (Chico, CA: Scholars Press, 1985), p. 79.

5. Richard Broholm, *Identifying Gifts and Arenas* (Newton Centre, MA: Center for the Ministry of the Laity, n.d.)

6. Tom Ott, *Equipping the Saints for Ministry: Bridging the Gap Between Faith and Work, a Church Planning Resource* (Newton Centre, MA: Center for the Ministry of the Laity, n.d.)

7. Warren Bennis and Burt Nanus, *Leaders: The Strategies for Taking Charge* (New York: Harper & Row, 1985), pp. 209-214.

8. The work of Edwin Friedman in *Generation to Generation* (New York: Guilford Press, 1985) is important here. As a member evolves into a leader and develops confidence, his or her learnings about him/herself carry over into other "family" settings. If in the church we can develop nonanxious leaders, we may do more for family life than all the counseling of a lifetime.

9. We based our approach on: United Church of Christ, Office for Church Life and Leadership, *The Ministry of Volunteers: A Guidebook for Churches* (1979).

10. William E. Diehl, op. cit.

11. James Anderson and Ezra Earl Jones, *The Ministry of the Laity* (San Francisco: Harper and Row, 1986).

12. Jackson W. Carroll, "Some Notes on Planned Social Change" (Hartford Seminary Foundation, unpublished manuscript, n.d.)

13. Matthew Fox, *Original Blessing* (Santa Fe: Bear & Co., 1983).

14. James Fenhagen, *Mutual Ministry* (New York: Seabury Press, 1977), p. 21.

15. Jackson W. Carroll, *Ministry as Reflective Practice* (Washington, DC: The Alban Institute, Inc., 1986), p. 15.

16. Robert A. Markus, "Work and Worker in Early Christianity" in *Work: Christian Thought and Practice,* ed. John M. Todd (Baltimore: Helicon Press, 1960).

17. Paolo Freire, interview by author, July, 1971 at Lima, Peru.

18. Hendrik Kraemer, *A Theology of the Laity* (Philadelphia: Westminster Press, 1958); *The Church for Others* (Geneva: World Council of Churches, 1967).

19. Barbara Wheeler, "What Kind of Leadership for Tomorrow's Churches?," *The Auburn News* (Spring 1985), p. 4.

20. For discussion of these themes, see Elizabeth Janeway, *Man's World, Woman's Place* (New York: Delta Books, 1971).

21. See Robert Bellah and others, *Habits of the Heart* (Berkeley: University of California Press, 1985).

22. *The Church for Others: A Quest for Structures for Missionary Congregations* (Geneva: World Council of Churches, 1967), pp. 18-19.

23. Thomas Wieser, *Planning for Mission* (New York: The U.S. Conference for the World Council of Churches, 1966), pp. 134-137.

BIBLIOGRAPHY

Anderson, James D. and Ezra Earl Jones. *The Ministry of the Laity*.
    San Francisco: Harper and Row, 1986.
Bellah, Robert, Richard Madsen, William M. Sullivan, Ann Swidler,
    and Steven M. Tipton. *Habits of the Heart*. New York: Harper
    and Row, 1985.
Bennis, Warren and Burt Nanus. *Leaders: The Strategies for Taking
    Charge*. New York: Harper & Row, 1985.
Broholm, Richard. *Identifying Gifts and Arenas*. Newton Centre,
    MA: Center for the Ministry of the Laity, n.d.
———, and David Morin-Specht. *Toward Claiming and Identifying
    our Ministry in the Workplace*. Newton Centre, MA: Center
    for the Ministry of the Laity, n.d.
Carroll, Jackson W., Carl S. Dudley, William McKinney, eds.
    Handbook for Congregational Studies. Nashville: Abingdon,
    1986.
Carroll, Jackson W. "Some Notes on Planned Social Change." n.p.
Diehl, William E.. *Thank God It's Monday*. Philadelphia: Fortress
    Press, 1982.
Dozier, Verna and Celia A. Hahn. *The Authority of the Laity*. Wash-
    ington: The Alban Institute, Inc., 1982.
Fenhagen, James C. *Mutual Ministry*. New York: Seabury, 1974.
Fox, Matthew. *Original Blessing*. Santa Fe, NM: Bear & Co., 1983.
Friedman, Edwin H. *Generation to Generation*. New York: Guilford
    Press, 1985.
Hahn, Celia A. *Lay Voices in an Open Church*. Washington: The
    Alban Institute, Inc., 1985.
———. *What Do I Have to Offer?* Washington, DC: The Alban Insti-
    tute, Inc., n.d.
Hastings, James, ed. *Encyclopedia of Religion and Ethics*. New
    York: Charles Scribners Sons, 1915. S.v. "Laity, Laymen," by
    A.J. Maclean.
Hulslander, Mac. "The Ministry of the Laity: Re-Thinking the Is-
    sues." Raleigh, NC: Clergy and Laity Together in Ministry, n.d.
———. "Included In: Laity and the Language of Ministry." Raleigh,
    NC: Clergy and Laity Together in Ministry, n.d.
Janeway, Elizabeth. *Man's World, Woman's Place*. New York: Delta
    Books, 1971.
Kraemer, Hendrik. *A Theology of the Laity*. Philadelphia: Westmin-
    ster Press, 1958.
McMakin, Jacqueline and Rhoda Nary. *Doorways to Christian
    Growth*. New York: Harper and Row, 1984.
Oldham, J.H. and W. A. Visser 't Hooft. *The Function of the
    Church*. World Council of Churches, 1937.

Ott, Tom. *Equipping the Saints for Ministry: Bridging the Gap Between Faith and Work, a Church Planning Resource.* Newton Center, MA: Center for the Ministry of the Laity, n.d.

Peck, George and John S. Hoffman. *Laity in Ministry.* Valley Forge: Judson Press, 1984.

Reber, Robert E. "Vocation and Vision: A New Look at the Ministry of the Laity," *The Auburn News,* Fall 1986.

Rhodes, Lynn. *Co-Creating: A Feminist Vision of Ministry.* Philadelphia: Westminster Press, 1987.

Rion, Michael. "The Responsible Manager: Ethics and Management in Christian Perspective." Prepublication copy of work in progress, 1988.

Rowthorn, Anne W. *The Liberation of the Laity.* Wilton, CT: Morehouse-Barlow, 1986.

Russell, Letty M. *The Future of Partnership.* Philadelphia: Westminster, 1979.

———. *Growth in Partnership.* Philadelphia: Westminster, 1981.

United Church of Christ. *The Ministry of Volunteers: A Guidebook for Churches.* United Church of Christ Office for Church Life and Leadership, 1979.

Wheeler, Barbara. "What Kind of Leadership for Tomorrow's Churches?" *The Auburn News,* Spring 1985.

World Council of Churches. *The Christian Hope and the Task of the Church.* New York: Harper, 1954.

———. *The Church for Others and The Church for the World.* Geneva: World Council of Churches, 1967.

———. *The Evanston Report.* New York: Harper, 1955.

———. *The New Delhi Report.* New York: Association Press, 1962.

The Alban Institute:
an invitation to membership

The Alban Institute, begun in 1974, believes that the congregation is essential to the task of equipping the people of God to minister in the church and the world. A multi-denominational membership organization, the Institute provides on-site training, educational programs, consulting, research, and publishing for hundreds of churches across the country.

The Alban Institute invites you to be a member of this partnership of laity, clergy and executives—a partnership that brings together people who are raising important questions about congregational life and people who are trying new solutions, making new discoveries, finding a new way of getting clear about the task of ministry. The Institute exists to provide you with the kinds of information and resources you need to support your ministries.

Join us now and enjoy these benefits:

Publications Discounts:

☐ 15% for Individual, Contributing and Supporting Members
☐ 40% for Judicatory and Seminary Executive members

Discounts on Training and Continuing Education

Action Information, a highly respected journal published 6 times a year, to keep you up to date on current issues and trends.

Write us for more information about how to join The Alban Institute, particularly about Congregational Memberships, in which 10 designated persons (25 for Supporting Congregational Members) receive all benefits of membership.

The Alban Institute, Inc.
4125 Nebraska Avenue NW
Washington, DC 20016